*Planning
Integrated
Units of Work
for Social
Education*

INTEGRATING

Socially

*Julie Hamston
and Kath Murdoch*

Heinemann
Portsmouth, NH

Dedicated to Janet — an inspiration to us all (JH)

. . . and to Marilyn and Keith who helped me see
the big picture (KM).

First published in 1996

Heinemann
A division of Reed Elsevier Inc.
361 Hanover Street Portsmouth, NH 03801-3959

Offices and agents throughout the world

ISBN 0 435 08899 8.

Published simultaneously in the United States
by Heinemann and in Australia by
Eleanor Curtain Publishing
906 Malvern Road
Armadale, Australia 3143

Production by Island Graphics
Edited by Ruth Siems
Text and cover design by David Constable
Typeset in 11/15pt New Baskerville by Island Graphics
Cover photographs by Sara Curtain
Printed in Australia

Contents

Acknowledgments

We wish to gratefully acknowledge the assistance of the teachers who trialled these units in their classrooms and gave us valuable feedback. We also thank them and their students for permission to use work samples throughout the book:

Steve Carter

Myf Van de Meene (year 5, Ivanhoe Girls Grammar School)

Sharon Fynmore

Tony Cerra

Kerry Hancock

Carmel Egan

Cathie Sutton

Margaret Rawlins (year 5/6, Meadow Heights Primary School)

Heather Bates (year 3–4, Brunswick North Primary School)

Rosa Guilano (year 4/5/6, Coburg Primary School)

Robin Galea (year 2–3, Coburg Primary School)

Glenn Beattie (year 5–6, Coburg Primary School)

Carol Guthrie (year 2–3, Laverton Plains Primary School)

Catherine Howells (year P–2, North Melbourne Primary School)

Lorraine Rabone

Judith Gurvich (year P–1, Wales Street Primary School, Thornbury)

Dianne Quigley

Helen Jordan

Sarah-Jane Fry

Gayle Ferguson (years 5 and 6, Springvale West Primary School)

We also thank the following people for their advice and assistance during the preparation of the manuscript:

Catherine Howells (Clifton Hill Primary School)

Julia Farrel

and Andrew Louey for assistance with diagrams.

Preface

This book provides teachers with a comprehensive and practical guide to developing integrated units of work for social education, incorporating a focus on language. It is based on our firm belief that effective teaching and learning depends on:

- a choice of curriculum content that is challenging, inclusive and dynamic
- a methodology which incorporates integration of curriculum and inquiry learning
- the selection of a wide range of texts (written, oral and visual) to resource units
- the development of a critical perspective in relation to these texts and the explicit teaching of genres to assist students in accessing, processing and presenting information and experience

The book is an amalgamation of our research interests and a result of the application of theory and practice in classrooms. Kath's work has focused on the professional development of teachers within the context of an integrated curriculum. By working alongside teachers in their classrooms, she has helped to implement an inquiry based methodology for integrating the curriculum across a wide range of classrooms. Central to her work is the relationship between choice of content and integrated curriculum. She has advocated that integrated curriculum must be based on significant content in order to be effective; content must enable students to develop 'big ideas' about the world (Pigdon & Woolley 1992). Kath's interests include the ways teachers can build their repertoire of *strategies* for effective teaching of integrated units—hence the focus on some key strategies in chapter 3.

Julie has worked directly with students to investigate the ways they see the world and how these can be identified, explored and reflected upon. She is most interested in the powerful influence of texts—written, oral and visual— on the ways in which we view the world and believes that students need to uncover the multiple messages contained within the texts. She believes that young learners and teachers need to develop a critical approach to texts so that they are able to discover the meanings they get *from* texts and the meanings they *take* to texts based on their own experiences of the world around them.

The units of work reflect these interests and our experience of working within a range of schools over recent years. The activities have been trialled in various classrooms and across various age levels, and we have benefited greatly from the feedback provided by teachers during this process.

This book is designed not only to provide teachers with a set of planned units but also as a guide for their own planning. Chapter 4 provides explicit assistance, but the units should be regarded as models. The seven topics cover a broad spectrum of social education content, but do not in themselves offer a complete program. Some guidance is provided in chapter 2 on the kind of content that should be covered in a comprehensive primary school social education curriculum.

The emphasis in this book is on aspects of society rather than aspects of the environment, although we recognise that the environment is a key component of social education. *Integrating Naturally* by Kath Murdoch (1992) outlines a further set of units with a focus on the environment.

The term **social education** has been used to define the field or area of curriculum central to this book. Whilst 'The studies of society' is a term used in many recent curriculum documents, we believe that social education continues to define the field in its broadest sense. *Integrating Socially* is concerned with a model of curriculum that actively engages the learner with the world and not merely with studying it for its own sake.

The term **language** has been used with the curriculum area of **English** in mind. However, we feel this book has wider application. Teachers of languages other than English or teachers of students who do not have English as their first language should be guided by the term 'language' and use this book to resource their teaching.

Figure 1 *Activities in the units may be used as part of a bilingual or language-other-than-English program*

CHAPTER 1

Social education through an integrated curriculum

THE NATURE OF SOCIAL EDUCATION
What is social education?

Social education enables teachers and learners to bring the world into the classroom. It provides opportunities for young learners to develop and apply understandings about communities, cultures and environments. It also encourages them to explore and clarify values and attitudes and to develop skills to investigate their world, discuss issues, solve problems, make decisions and work cooperatively with others. Importantly, social education encourages young learners to act on the understandings, values and skills they have developed about the world around them.

In view of the steady globalisation of all aspects of life, the aim of a social education program should be to develop young learners who have a sense of themselves as active participants in the global network; young citizens who have the knowledge, skills, values and decision-making capacities to navigate the complexities of contemporary life.

Learning for active participation

Social education as an area of curriculum has evolved a great deal in recent decades. There is now a strong emphasis on *taking action*, whereby learners are encouraged to apply the knowledge, skills, and values they have developed about the world around them to their daily lives and the lives of others. This emphasis helps to ensure that social education is an active process, encouraging learners to practise what they have learnt in personal, local and global domains.

Acting on what has been learnt, however, involves doing what is practical, achievable and realistic. For students at the primary level, taking action does not mean countless letters of protest to the government or organising demonstrations; rather, it involves them taking small steps to improve the quality of their day-to-day lives. It is essential that students feel a sense of achievement in what they have done, whether this means sharing their work with another class or creating a list of recommendations for the junior school council. Taking action provides students with opportunities to feel positive and empowered rather than overwhelmed and powerless in the face of rapid social change.

Choosing content for social education

Becoming effective, active citizens depends on the development of an awareness and understanding about the 'way the world works'. Young learners need to develop inclusive world views and a greater capacity to live with difference, and to challenge interpretations of the world that may be narrow in focus, inaccurate or even discriminatory. The inclusion of a unit of work on an Asian country is an attempt to address the development of more inclusive world views and to provide learners with alternative perspectives on the nature of the world.

Choice of significant content is determined by 'big ideas about the world' that are important for young learners to explore. These include key perspectives such as *globalism, citizenship, diversity, heritage,* and *decision-making* (see below). The perspectives provide a broad reference for content selection, indicating some essential understandings to be developed about the world as it is, as it has been, and how it may be in the future. Central to the selection of content and subsequent planning are the fundamental questions:

What view(s) of the world am I presenting to students?

Whose world am I bringing in to the classroom?

Am I developing the understanding that there are many ways of viewing the world?

Am I exposing my students to this diversity?

Key perspectives

Social education programs should reflect and incorporate current and future issues and trends within the global society. It is important that schools regularly review their programs in the light of these changing trends and perspectives. Teachers need to continually ask themselves:

What are the significant ideas and experiences in which we should be engaging students?

What kind of world will they move into as young adults? How can we prepare them for an active and critical role in that world?

Ultimately, our curriculum planning should enable students to relate their knowledge and inquiry skills to real life-contexts. The numerous perspectives within this context are summarised on the following pages.

MAKING CHOICES AND TAKING ACTION

Helping young people to develop the skills and understandings required to make informed choices in their daily lives. Involving them in learning through action and developing the confidence and competence to participate as *active citizens*. Understanding the powerful influences (such as the media, the peer group) that affect decision-making.

IMAGINING AND CONSTRUCTING THE FUTURE

Providing young people with the means to 'think ahead'—to develop the capacity to envisage probable, possible and preferable futures and the understandings and skills which allow them to play an active role in constructing the future. Instilling the confidence to become an active citizen in the society that will be theirs.

THINKING CRITICALLY

Encouraging young people to 'think more deeply' about the way the world works and to view experiences and ideas from a range of perspectives. To develop inclusive world views and the understanding that truth is a relative notion. To look behind and beyond the surface of any issue. To ask the questions: What is really going on here? Whose view of the world is this? Is this view the same for all people? Do I have to agree with this view of the world? In what ways do I view the world? Where do these views of the world come from?

ECOLOGICAL SUSTAINABILITY

Helping young people to recognise the range of ways in which living things depend on the natural environment for their survival and, in turn, the ways in which humans impact on that environment. Developing a commitment to maintaining the environment as the life source for all living things and recognising the intrinsic value of the natural environment.

THE GLOBAL SOCIETY

Helping young people to understand that they are part of a global, interdependent network of human beings, technologies and systems. That what people do in a community, and as a nation, affects and is affected by others across the world.

INDIVIDUAL POTENTIAL

Encouraging in young people a strong sense of themselves as active members of their immediate and wider community. Fostering a sense of hope, aspiration, confidence and personal achievement.

DIVERSITY AND DIFFERENCE

Helping young people to understand that diversity is integral to life within the global community and that all individuals need to learn to live and work with difference.

LIVING WITH UNCERTAINTY

Developing young people who have the confidence to live with change in a rapidly expanding global community. To recognise that this uncertainty contains possibility as well as the need for concern.

JUSTICE, RIGHTS AND RESPONSIBILITIES

Developing an awareness of fundamental human rights for all people. To recognise that individuals and groups of people must exercise responsibility in ensuring that the rights of one do not work against the rights of others.

CULTURAL HERITAGE

Helping young people to understand and appreciate the ways in which diverse cultures have influenced and continue to shape their society, lifestyles and the ways they view the world. Exploring and valuing their own cultural heritage.

TIME, PLACE AND SPACE

Developing an awareness of continuity and change. Understanding the nature of change at both the local and global levels. Developing an insight into the patterns and processes that accompany change in a diversity of contexts, and an understanding of the ways in which historical events shape the present and the future. Understanding the relationship between geographical and natural features and the ways in which they influence the organisation of local and global communities.

INDIGENOUS PEOPLE

Helping young people to develop a clearer understanding and appreciation of the experiences of indigenous people across the world and then, more specifically, of the nature of issues surrounding the culture of indigenous people within their own nation. Developing the notion of 'sharing cultures'.

CHANGING LIFESTYLES—WORK AND LEISURE

Developing in young people the skills and understandings needed to adjust to the changing balance between and nature of work and leisure.

SPIRITUALITY

Acknowledging that effective citizenship in the global community depends on the continued development of the *self* in relation to other people, the natural and physical environments and placement in time. Developing the capacity to reflect deeply, to probe and question; working towards an inner peacefulness.

DEVELOPING VALUES

Developing the understanding that some values are shared and assist any group or society to function and work together and that a range of individual or subjective values exist within the local and global community. To assist young people to develop the capacity to explore and clarify personal value positions and identify with the value positions of others.

SOCIAL EDUCATION AND AN INTEGRATED CURRICULUM

We do not just sit and wait for the world to impinge on us. We try to actively interpret it, to make sense of it. We grapple with it, we construe it intellectually, we represent it ourselves. (Donaldson 1978)

The 'connectedness of things'

The study of society provides a powerful context within which students can develop skills and understandings across the curriculum and through which they can come to understand the 'connectedness of things'. We believe that an integrated approach is the most effective means by which social education can be manifested in the classroom: it provides greater purpose and meaning in the daily experience of teaching and learning and acknowledges the complex links that connect people with each other and with the planet. The real world is not fragmented or boxed into separate compartments. Life is a complex mix of interrelated experiences—each action affects another—and people depend on each other and on the planet for their very survival. Our curriculum should acknowledge and reflect the nature of this connectedness.

Why integrate?

The demand on teachers to accommodate seemingly endless additions to the school curriculum calls for a more unified and integrated approach to planning. As our information base expands and our access to that information increases there is a need to develop a curriculum that is connected by unifying ideas—that draws common threads together. The fragmentation of the curriculum through separate treatment of traditional subjects may create a learning context which is inflexible, teacher driven, lacking in relevance to the student and shallow in its treatment of the content.

An effective integrated curriculum allows teachers and students to work more efficiently and is one way of loosening the pressure on teachers as they struggle to achieve an impossible balancing act—trying to find enough hours in their week to 'fit it all in'.

THE KEY REASONS

We believe an integrated approach is the most valid way to approach social education in our schools for a number of key reasons. In summary, an integrated curriculum:

- loosens the pressure created by rigid timetables and a stop-start curriculum, assisting teachers and students to use and manage their time more productively
- assists students and teachers to develop more efficient means of gathering, organising and processing the information increasingly available to us on a global as well as a local level
- helps deal with a curriculum that is 'bulging at the seams' and challenges teachers to develop ways in which students can reorganise and bring the pieces together
- helps us focus on the 'big ideas' rather than trivialising the content of our programs
- makes more sense to the child's (and teacher's) day by providing a flow of learning rather than a stop–start approach
- develops a sense of community
- caters more successfully for individual differences and for the interests and needs of the learner
- encourages students to consider *how* they learn while developing important concepts and understandings
- provides genuine and rich contexts for developing a range of skills and understandings

USING AN INQUIRY APPROACH

An effective integrated curriculum should consider not only the connections across learning areas but also the way in which students learn. The units in this book are based on an inquiry theory of learning that acknowledges the key role of the student in setting directions and actively participating in the construction of learning experiences.

Developing critical understandings about the social world should be seen as a shared enterprise between teacher and learner; we have developed these units with a belief that curriculum should be interpretive and transformative. Our view of the teacher's role is not simply one of passing on a certain 'body of knowledge' to students. Instead, the units are designed to engage teachers and learners in shared investigations — teaching and learning are viewed as a two-way process.

Inquiry learning is a widely accepted methodology that has long been advocated as fundamental to social education. It involves a strong emphasis on student-centred, active learning and on the *process* of investigating as much as the product. The prior knowledge and experience of the student are the starting points for investigations and students are encouraged to actively participate in determining ways in which they will gather and process new ideas. The approach encourages students, through active investigation, to unify, rather than separate knowledge as they move from the acquisition of facts to the development of broader concepts and generalisations. It opens up channels of investigation which subject-specific curriculum may otherwise close and emphasises the learning of fundamental principles and concepts—the 'big ideas'.

A planning model

Opportunities to integrate curriculum often arise simply within the informal, spontaneous fabric of the school day—planning a class excursion, sorting out a schoolyard conflict, taking up an issue that has been reported in the media, and so on. Indeed, many of the key purposes of social education can be met simply through the way in which we respond to and utilise these incidental moments. Our purposes can also be met through careful organisation of classroom routines and procedures that promote equity, participation, communication and cooperation.

There remain, however, many aspects of social education that need to become a part of our planned curriculum. We have found that inquiry-based, integrated units of work are effective vehicles for social education and the model we have used in this book, drawing on the work of Pigdon and Woolley (1992), provides a useful structure for planning.

Figure 2 *A model of integrated learning*

Information	Nature of activity	Subjects involved
Facts	*Prior knowledge* • making predictions • asking questions	
	Shared experiences • observation • collecting information /data	*Learning about* • social education • science • environmental education • personal development • technology studies
Concepts	*Processing information* • listing • grouping • categorising • classifying • labelling • organising ideas	*Learning through* • language • art • drama • mathematics • movement • music
Generalisations	*Synthesysing* • making statements • generalising • looking for relationships	*Learning about* • social education • science • environmental education • personal development • technology studies

Further information	*Refinement and extension of knowledge*
	• elaborating
	• justifying
	• reflecting

In this model, curriculum areas such as language, drama, music, art and mathematics are defined as process areas which are used to explore, question, refine and present content (drawn, in this case, from social education) within an inquiry framework. In contrast to a thematic model, attention is given to the nature of learning, the types of activities which can be sequenced to enhance learning, and the nature of planning and teaching which facilitates learning (see figure 4).

The model reflects the process of learning and its sequential journey from the acquisition of facts to the formation of generalisations while allowing curriculum areas to integrate as they become useful or appropriate through the various stages of inquiry. These stages and their purposes are outlined below (Murdoch 1992; Pigdon & Woolley 1992). While it is important to recognise the purposes in each stage, units of work will not always flow neatly from one stage to the next. Activities will overlap in their purposes and outcomes. These stages do, however, help teachers to ask the question: For what purpose am I doing this activity?

TUNING IN

Activities should:

- provide students with opportunities to become engaged with the topic
- ascertain the students' initial curiosity about the topic
- allow students to share their personal experience of the topic

PREPARING TO FIND OUT

Activities should:

- establish what the students already know about the topic
- provide the students with a focus for the forthcoming experience
- help in the planning of further experience and activities

FINDING OUT

Activities should:

- further stimulate the students' curiosity
- provide new information which may answer some of the students' earlier questions
- raise other questions for the students to explore in the future
- challenge the students' knowledge, beliefs and values
- help students to make sense of further activities and experiences which have been planned for them

SORTING OUT

Activities should:

- provide students with concrete means of sorting out and representing information and ideas arising from the 'finding-out' stage
- provide students with the opportunity to process the information they have gathered and present this in a number of ways
- allow for a diverse range of outcomes

GOING FURTHER

Activities should:

- extend and challenge students' understanding about the topic
- provide more information in order to broaden the range of understandings available to the students

MAKING CONNECTIONS

Activities should:

- help students draw conclusions about what they have learnt
- provide opportunities for reflection both on what has been learnt and on the learning process itself

TAKING ACTION

Activities should:

- assist students to make links between their understandings and their experience in the real world
- enable students to make choices and develop the belief that they can be effective participants in society
- provide further insight into students' understandings for future unit planning

MORE THAN THEMES

In recent decades, the treatment of social education in schools has often been carried out using a thematic approach. The use of themes was seen as a way of making the curriculum more cohesive and helping learners to make some connections between various subject areas. Themes, however, were often shallow in nature and connections between curriculum areas could be forced or artificial. Many thematic units were a smorgasbord of activities loosely built around a topic rather than a careful selection of activities designed to gradually build understandings about the social world.

The units in this book seek to move teachers beyond a thematic approach to a more genuinely integrated approach that guides students through an explicit sequence of learning in topic areas that deal with significant and challenging issues. There is no attempt to use all curriculum areas in each unit of work; instead we have selected those that offer the most appropriate ways to help students gather or sort data as they move towards under-standings. Figure 4 summarises some key differences between a thematic and an integrated approach to social education.

PULLING THE THREADS TOGETHER

This is essentially a book about classroom practice. What we have presented in this chapter is an overview of the theory that guides the practice shared in the following pages. In summary, we believe social education is best manifested in a curriculum that:

- is based on ideas and **topics of substance and significance**
- emphasises the **connectedness** of knowledge and unifies curriculum
- assists the learner in understand **'big ideas'** rather than isolated facts
- emphasises the **process** of learning as well as the **content**
- develops the learner's **skills** in context
- values the **experiences, prior knowledge and interests** of the learner
- creates **sustained learning experiences** rather than one-off unrelated lessons
- emphasises **open-ended** rather than limiting activities
- allows the learner some degree of **choice** within their investigations
- draws on **real life experiences and issues**
- encourages the growth of **critical thinking and reflection**
- empowers the learner **to act** on his/her understanding
- makes use of a wide **range of 'texts'** to develop students' understandings, skills and values
- encourages a **critical approach** to reading texts
- provides opportunities for developing a broad repertoire of written and oral language skills through a **focus on genre**

Figure 3 *Bringing the world into the classroom*

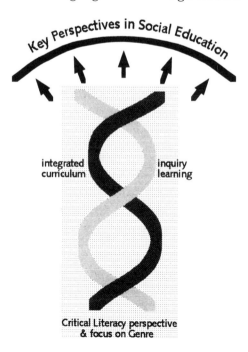

Thematic units	Inquiry-based integrated units
Topics are often selected at random and are based on language themes (color, pirates, fantasy, etc). Topic selection is often process rather then content driven.	Topics are selected to develop significant understandings about society. This content 'drives' the unit. Processes are used in a meaningful context. Topics are seen as vehicles for the gradual development of big ideas about society.
Activities are often only loosely linked to the topic: a transport theme may involve students in making a graph of the different colored cars in the carpark. The learning about transport itself is minimal.	Activities are designed to develop planned **understandings** about the topic. The teacher asks: How will this activity help to develop and challenge students' understandings about this topic?
Attempts are made to include *every* area of the curriculum in each theme, often resulting in forced rather than genuine links. The teacher may ask, for example: How can I make maths fit into this theme.	The study of society drives the teacher's planning and forms the content of the unit. Maths, language, art and other process areas are selected according to the extent to which they can be purposefully used by the learner. The students and teacher ask, for example: What is the most effective way we could present this data?
There is no necessary sequence of activities. They tend to be discrete and unconnected and are able to be carried out in random order.	Activities are developed along an inquiry model of teaching and learning. Units move through a broad **sequence of stages.**
Themes are largely driven by the various separate curriculum areas: English and mathematics become the focus rather than learning about the social world.	The unit merges areas of the curriculum together in **purposeful** ways.
Themes are often planned as the whole classroom program: all or most activities done during the course of the week are under the umbrella of one topic.	Integrated units are a significant part of the classroom program. Other regular routines will continue to operate alongside them and there will be times when the teacher will 'step out' of the unit to focus on a particular skill or concept or other curriculum area.
Student choice and input may be very limited within a theme; activities are planned and directed by the teacher. On the other hand, some thematic approaches take the opposite view and build the activities almost entirely around student interest, often including the choice of topic itself.	Teachers consider both the **interests** and **needs** of students in their planning. A degree of choice exists for the learner but this is negotiated with other students and with the teacher.

Figure 4 *Key differences between a thematic and an integrated approach to social education*

CHAPTER 2

About the units of work

THE FRAMEWORK

The units of work have been designed using an inquiry-based, integrated approach to curriculum. Each unit begins by ascertaining students' own experiences and understandings about the topic. A series of investigative activities is then suggested to enable students to gather new ideas and information. Then a range of activities are outlined to help students to sort out and make sense of this new information. In the latter stages of each unit, activities are suggested to help students reflect on, generalise and analyse their new understandings and to put them into action in some way.

Although this broad sequence is repeated in each unit, the content, strategies, resources and experiences are diverse. We have selected a range of topics and have pitched the units at different age levels to ensure this diversity. Together, the units should provide a comprehensive repertoire for planning, teaching and assessment.

Each unit has been trialled in the classroom—working with a variety of age levels, school settings and teachers. Feedback from teachers and students has helped us to refine our plans and provide what we hope is a clear and practical framework to assist other teachers in their own planning.

USING THE UNITS

These units can be used in a number of ways. They will be of most benefit to teachers who wish to implement a sustained sequence of activities following the stages identified in chapter 1. At each stage, several activities are suggested from which you are encouraged to select the most appropriate for your purposes. We would not expect all the activities in each stage of a unit to be used. Alternatively, the activities may be used to add to or complement planning in other areas or on other topics. Although the activities are designed to be taught within the context of the unit as written, many of them would stand alone if needed for other specific teaching purposes.

The units may be used by a team of teachers within and across class/age levels. There is a lot of choice at each stage, allowing teachers to select their own sequence of activities and to respond to students' interests and needs.

Planning menus are provided to assist in selecting and recording activities from the more detailed plans. Finally, the units provide models for your own planning using other topics (see chapter 4).

Resourcing the units

The resources suggested are, on the whole, general rather than specific. Schools and the context in which they exist vary widely as does the availability of some resources—particularly in remote areas. There is a strong emphasis in the units on gathering raw data; interviews, surveys and observations feature strongly, as these methods develop important skills and ensure that the exploration of the topic is grounded in a relevant context. The students and their local community are important resources in each unit.

Some children's literature is suggested in several units, as are examples of excursion venues, types of video and computer material. You will need to investigate what is available in your school and local area, and it is often a good idea to establish networks between schools in order to share resources.

Ensure that students experience various forms in which information can be accessed, including: direct experience (excursions), hearing from others (interviews and guest speakers), video, computer programs (Internet, use of CD-ROM packages), drawings, paintings and other visual images, books (fiction and nonfiction), tapes, kits, artefacts, slides, charts and maps, journals, magazines and newspapers. You may find the following criteria useful when selecting specific resources. They should be:

- relevant to understandings
- inclusive in terms of gender, age and ethnicity
- varied in type
- gathered by students as well as by the teacher
- available for revisiting by students throughout the unit

ADAPTING THE UNITS

Each unit of work is targeted at a particular age range (lower primary: 5–8 year olds, middle to upper primary: 9–11 year olds, upper primary to lower secondary: 12–14 year olds). These are suggested age ranges only and it is expected that teachers will be able to modify the activities to suit the needs and abilities of the students with whom they are working. There is a range of activities within each stage from simple to more complex, and this will allow selection on the basis of need, both within the class as well as across the school. Many of the units have been used with a range of age levels.

The unit topics are based on the key perspectives of social education as outlined in chapter 1 and embrace content that we believe is of relevance and significance to all students. Some topics, however, may require different emphases according to the needs and priorities of a particular school community. We would encourage you to explore ways in which content can be adjusted to relate to the context in which you are working.

Figure 5 *Computers are valuable tools for investigating, sorting and presenting data*

WHAT ABOUT ASSESSMENT?

Rather than being a task carried out at the end of each unit, assessment is viewed as integral to the entire unit sequence. Each activity should be regarded as a context for assessment of student learning. The approach to assessment underpinning these units is based on the following six principles:

1 The fundamental purpose of assessment is to improve student learning.
2 Assessment should focus on the development of the individual learner rather than on comparisons between learners.
3 Assessment strategies should cater for a range of learning styles within a class, and should not be limited to written tasks.
4 Students should be active participants in the assessment process and be conscious of their strengths and the areas in which they need to improve.
5 Within an integrated curriculum, assessment might occur at multiple levels and across curriculum areas. For example, a role-play activity may provide an opportunity for assessment of understanding about the topic, of oral language skills, of understanding of persuasive genre and of the ability to work in a small group.
6 Assessment should inform subsequent program planning at both an individual and a whole class level.

When planning and implementing a unit of work, make clear decisions about what you will focus on in assessing learning. The units provide an opportunity for *many* skills and understandings to be observed but it is impractical and unwieldy to attempt to focus on too much. We encourage you to devise a simple assessment plan that forecasts areas to be assessed over subsequent weeks. In planning for assessment, student growth in the following should be considered:

• understandings about the topic
• development of skills
• exploration and clarification of values
• specific learning outcomes across curriculum areas

- use of language in relation to content
- ability to reflect on learning and to see purposes behind activities
- ability to use and critically analyse a range of texts
- ability to work cooperatively with others
- approach to learning (independence, confidence, participation, enthusiasm)

In each unit, a list of understandings and specific outcomes for social education and language are provided to assist teachers in planning for assessment.

Assessment strategies

Each stage in the inquiry sequence provides information about student learning. There are, however, two stages in each unit that are critical to assessment: the **preparing to find out** stage and the **making connections** stage. Work that is carried out in these stages will assist teachers and students to monitor growth and to see concrete examples of the way ideas have been refined or changed through the unit sequence. Work samples should be retained for this purpose.

There are several strategies used often in these units that are particularly helpful for 'getting inside the learner's head'. These strategies, many of which are explained in more depth in chapter 3, are:

- concept mapping
- effects wheels
- writing or drawing generalisations
- learning logs
- learning maps
- self-assessment
- peer assessment
- oral interviews (recorded onto tape and then revisited later in the unit)
- analysis of art work
- written responses to key questions (early and late in the unit)
- revisiting early work and making changes
- collection of relevant work samples for analysis

CRITICAL LITERACY AND GENRE

Teachers bring the world into the classroom through texts: written texts such as literature, diary extracts, historical records; visual texts such as photographs, television, video; and oral texts such as discussions, interviews, or the viewpoints of a guest speaker. A rich variety of texts enhances a social education program and provides students with 'windows' to the world. Ensure that the texts you select to 'bring the world into the classroom' provide students with varied and challenging perspectives.

It is essential, however, that in developing inclusive views about the world,

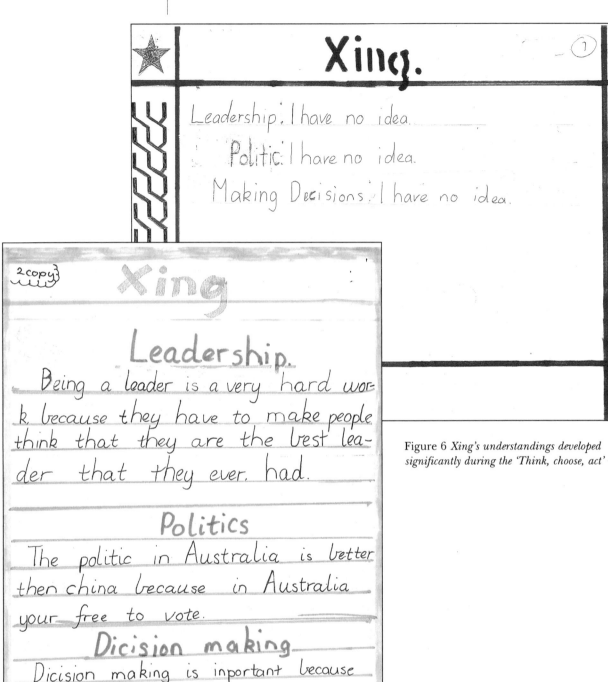

Figure 6 *Xing's understandings developed significantly during the 'Think, choose, act' unit*

young learners are encouraged to 'read' these texts critically and uncover the social and cultural meanings embedded within them. For example, within a unit of work on local history, students might read diary extracts of people who lived in the area long ago. These extracts could be examined for similarities and differences in language used then and now, for a variety of viewpoints on the same event, or to uncover meanings about the ways of life for people of different social status and so on.

The study of society is also useful to the exploration of different **types of texts,** or **genres,** including recounts, explanations, arguments or persuasions, reports, narratives, instructions or procedures. For example, exploring the ways in which a factual recount of the local area is structured enables students to understand the relationship between the purpose of the recount, the intended audience, and the way in which the recount is written or spoken. Importantly, students explore the way different views of the world can influence a personal recount of a particular event in time—adding to their overall understanding of the ways in which history can be constructed.

A detailed examination of the genre used to access information and experience and the genre used to process this information and experience can complement any unit of work. For example, students might view a range of photographs of women and men in a unit of work on advertising to discover how advertisements use language to construct particular images of women and men. At the end of the unit, students could develop argumentative writing to demonstrate their understandings of the power of advertising.

Each unit of work has been developed with the important relationship between language and social education in mind. Central to each unit is:
- a focus on using a range of written, spoken and visual texts to 'bring the world into the classroom'
- a focus on exploring text types or genres—the relationship between purpose, audience and the structure of the text
- opportunities for exploring the social and cultural meanings embedded within texts—what the text says to the reader and what the reader brings to the text from their own experience

In general terms, we have drawn on critical literacy theory and genre theory to inform this emphasis on the social and cultural nature of language and literacy. Much debate exists in Australia about the differing positions on language and literacy taken by proponents of genre theory and critical literacy. We believe that genre theory need not be seen in direct opposition to the aims of critical literacy, provided that the teaching of genre does not assume these forms of writing to be dominant *and fixed.* Students need access to the dominant forms of writing and make use of them, but they must also be encouraged to render these forms of writing 'problematic' and open to transformation and change. Examples of the structures and features of different genres have been provided, but teachers are encouraged to see these as *models* of different genres subject to social and historical change. We are advocating that students need to be encouraged to 'critically read' the genres they are learning to control.

CHAPTER 3

Useful strategies for social education

The following strategies are suggested for use throughout the units in this book. They are generic in nature and can be used and modified across a wide range of topics and age levels. Importantly, they provide students with different 'ways of learning'. Strategies for problem-solving, organising and sorting, thinking creatively, and reflecting can be used in many different aspects of the school curriculum and applied to life beyond school. Teachers are encouraged to build these strategies into their own units of work.

It is essential that each strategy is actually **taught** to the students—that it is modelled by teachers with opportunities provided for rehearsal and practice. By repeating the strategy a number of times and using it in different units, students will become increasingly familiar with the strategy itself, and gradually able to attend more to the content.

Students should become familiar with the names of the strategies they are using. This can be achieved by listing the strategies as they are introduced, perhaps with instructions on each procedure to which students can refer. Encourage them to reflect on the success of each strategy: How did it help them learn? How might it be useful in another context? What aspects need to be worked on for next time?

Consensus 1–3–6

PURPOSE

- to develop skills in cooperative decision-making
- to generate both a personal and a group list of ideas
- to encourage sharing of ideas and to learn from one another

PROCEDURE

Step 1: Individually, students generate a list of ideas around a certain topic. These may be words, pictures, sentences or questions. Give students a time limit in which to complete the task and, perhaps, limit the number of items you wish them to list.

Step 2: Students now work in groups of three to combine their lists into one. Ideas are discussed, modified, justified, included, or rejected until a list is agreed upon. Again a limit on time and the number of items can be helpful.

Step 3: Two trios now get together and repeat the process using the two lists each group has generated. The final list generated by each group of six may be written on large sheets of butchers paper and displayed for discussion.

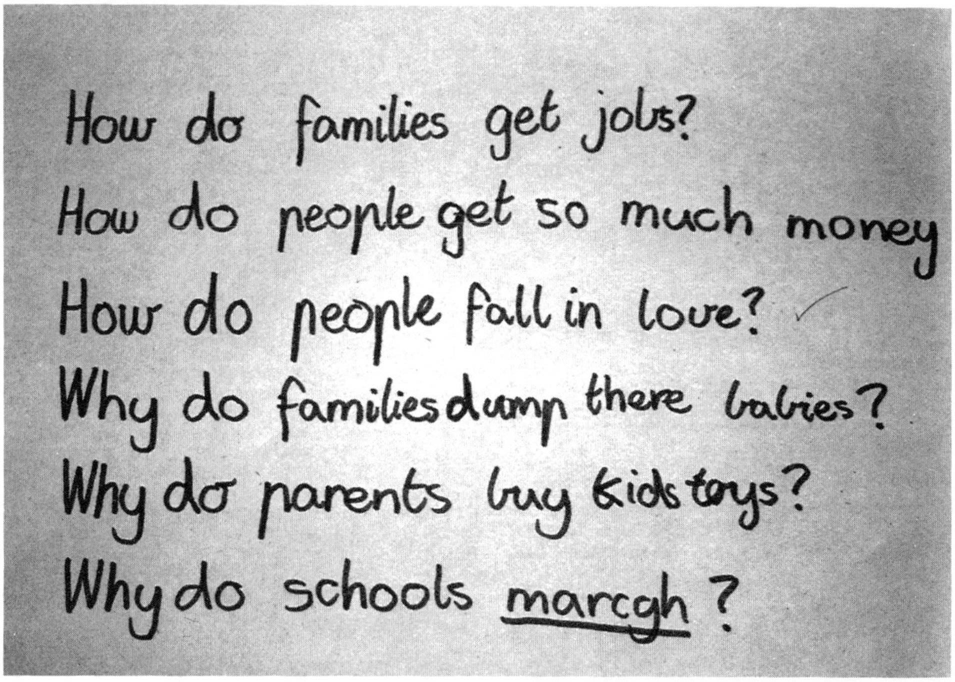

Figure 7 *A list of questions generated through the 1–3–6 strategy*

How do families get jobs?
How do people get so much money
How do people fall in love? ✓
Why do families dump there babies?
Why do parents buy kids toys?
Why do schools <u>marcgh</u>?

NOTES
- For younger students—or those less experienced in cooperative work—this procedure can be done using 1–2 or 1–2–4 groupings.
- Individual lists can be retained by the teacher for assessment purposes.
- Encourage students to reflect on the process of coming to a consensus.
- The activity can be followed by asking each group to prioritise their ideas.
- Revisit initial lists later in the unit and make any changes or modifications in the light of new understandings.

Interviews and surveys

PURPOSE
- to assist students in gathering information about the topic
- to develop skills of formulating questions, gathering and recording data
- to develop communication skills: oral language and active listening
- to develop the understanding that we can learn from the experience of others

PROCEDURE
Interviews can be conducted in a range of ways. Here is a suggested sequence of teaching steps for students who are relatively new to the strategy:
Step 1: Ask students what they know about interviews and what they are used for.

Step 2: View or listen to various interviews from television or radio. Ask students: What was the role of the interviewer? What was the role of the interviewee? How do you think they both felt? What information was the interviewer trying to gather? How effective were the questions?

Step 3: Students practise interviewing each other. Alternatively, you could conduct impromptu interviews with different students. Base interviews on issues or experiences with which students are familiar.

Step 4: Brainstorm questions for the interview.

Step 5: Rehearse introductions and explanations. How can we make the person feel at ease? How should we thank them? How will we record the information?

Figure 8 *A list of questions developed for an interview*

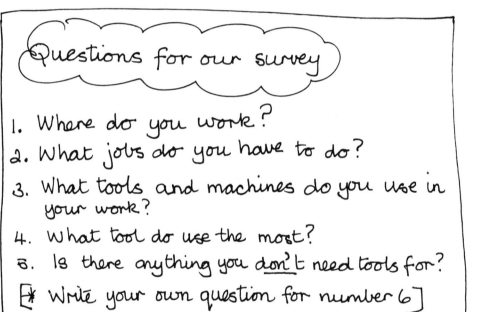

Questions for our survey

1. Where do you work?
2. What jobs do you have to do?
3. What tools and machines do you use in your work?
4. What tool do use the most?
5. Is there anything you don't need tools for?
[* Write your own question for number 6]

NOTES

• Interviews are a useful way of helping students to develop efficient note-taking techniques. Practise taking notes of key points.

• Interviews can be re-created in the classroom as a role-play exercise.

• Use an old or toy microphone to add some interest and motivation to interview practice.

• Record interviews between students and ask them to analyse their questioning style and responses.

People bingo

PURPOSE

• to tune students into a topic

• to find out about students' experiences or prior knowledge

• to help students to get to know one another

• to develop a sense of community in the class

PROCEDURE

Step 1: Design a sheet with several boxes, each containing a sentence beginning' Find someone who ...', for example 'Find someone who was born in another country.'

Step 2: Students move around the room and attempt to get a different signature in each box, according to the questions. Encourage students to talk with each other as they go. They should hear the response from others, not just collect signatures.

Step 3: Stop the activity once most sheets are completed and seat everyone in a circle.

Step 4: Ask students to introduce others to the group by way of the information they found out about them.

NOTES

• This should not be turned into a competition for the most signatures as this defeats the purpose of the activity.

• Reflect on the activity and note those students who have very few signatures. Did they, in fact, spend all their time helping others? Who finished quickly? Why?

• Information from the sheets could be used to develop a profile of each student in relation to that topic.

• Beginning readers can be assisted by including pictures in the boxes to remind them about the meaning of the sentences.

Research contracts

PURPOSE

• to encourage students to work efficiently and independently

• to allow individuals or small groups to follow a particular path of interest

• to gather a range of data to bring back to the class as a whole

PROCEDURE

Step 1: Help students select sub-topics within the broader topic that the class is working on. These can often be triggered by the questions or issues raised at the beginning of the unit: 'What would you like to find out more about?'

Step 2: Organise students into pairs or small groups. Each is responsible for a different sub-topic.

Step 3: Students write a list of questions they wish to explore. (These can be drafted and then conferenced with others.)

Step 4: Brainstorm then select ways that information will be gathered. If necessary, allocate different tasks to different group members (e.g. reading, watching video material, visiting a place, interviewing people).

Step 5: Consider how which information will be recorded and then presented to others (e.g. posters, oral presentations, video tapes, big books, song).

Figure 9 *An example of a list of students' questions*

> • What is the oldest house in our neigbourhood?
>
> • What did our neighbourhood look like 100 years ago?
>
> • How did people get from one place to another?
>
> • What did people wear in the olden days?

Step 6: The group develops a timeline, predicting when each stage of the project might be completed and by whom.

Step 7: Establish a series of group meeting times and also set aside special times when groups make appointments for progress reports to the class or to the teacher.

Step 8: Teacher and students sign the contract, once agreed.

NOTES

- Research contracts will vary across topics, schools, age levels, etc. The above steps and examples are one way of negotiating a research contract with students. They are best developed once the unit is well under way and a basic understanding of the topic has been gained.

De Bono's 6 thinking hats

PURPOSE

- to encourage students to see issues from a range of perspectives
- to develop students' skills of thinking in different ways
- to help students explore and clarify values

PROCEDURE

Again, the procedure for using the 6 thinking hats is not fixed and will vary according to the specific purpose, topic and familiarity with each hat. The steps below are a broad outline only.

Step 1: Introduce the nature of the 'hats' one at a time and practise using the hat in response to issues and events throughout the day. For example: What would a red-hat thinker say to this? Let's put our red hats on after that story ... how do you feel?

Step 2: Once students are familiar with the nature of each hat, they can use them in all sorts of ways. Try giving different groups a different color. Each group must respond to an issue/question/problem according to that hat's perspective. They document their ideas on large sheets of paper.

Step 3: The sheets of paper are passed on until every group has written something down.

Step 4: Students are asked to think about the hat they most and least identify with and why.

NOTES

- Use actual colored hats to help the activity become more concrete. Try making a set of paper hats that can be used at any time during the day.
- Develop characters for role play around the ideas generated from the 6 hats activities.
- Draw/paint/ mime responses using the hats as a guide.

Watch this space

PURPOSE

- to actively involve students in a whole class discussion of an issue or topic
- to encourage active listening and clear oral communication
- to share ideas and opinions

PROCEDURE

Step 1: Set up two circles of chairs or cushions— a small inner circle of about 6, and an outer circle.

Step 2: A small group self-selects or is selected to begin in the inner circle. They are given a particular topic to discuss. Other students sit in the outer circle and observe the discussion for a set period of time but may not interrupt.

Step 3: Students in the outer circle who wish to have a say must raise their hand. When given the signal by the teacher, selected individuals from the outer circle may tap someone on the shoulder in the inner circle who must then vacate their chair. Once the space is vacated, they join the inner circle to enter the discussion.

Step 4: Students who have been largely observing the discussion report back on what they noticed about issues raised and discussion strategies used.

NOTES

- Teachers play an important managerial role in implementing this strategy.
- Students may be allowed to vacate an inner space voluntarily should they have little to add to the discussion.
- A fishbowl discussion can also be used where the two circles remain fixed and students in the outer circle are given specific observation points (e.g. 'Observe the way people use their body language during a discussion').

Conversation counters

PURPOSE

- to encourage greater equity and participation in group discussions
- to help students to learn how to take turns and to wait for others

PROCEDURE

Step 1: Give each student in the group a set of approximately 3–4 conversation counters (e.g. blocks or beads) and place a bowl in the middle of the discussion circle. Each time a student wishes to talk they must give up one of their conversation counters. Students should attempt to use up all their counters during the course of the discussion.

Step 2: Proceed with the discussion.

Step 3: Discuss: How did that change the way we talk as a large group? Who used up their conversation counters quickly? Why? Who still has most of their counters? Why?

NOTES

- The same effect can be achieved using a talking stick. This is a particular object, such as a glitter covered stick, that is passed to the student who wishes to speak. Only those with the talking stick can speak. A rule can be established that only allows the stick to be passed to each person once.
- Conversation counters can be used in cooperative group work.

Structured brainstorms

PURPOSE

- to gather information about students' prior knowledge on a topic
- to pool ideas and share with others
- to help set directions for an investigation

PROCEDURE

Step 1: Provide focus questions about the topic to individuals or small groups and ask them to brainstorm their thoughts and ideas in response.

Step 2: Share the lists in larger groups or as a class. Note common items, contradictory items, etc. Circle key words and place a question mark next to those that cause debate or controversy. These can be used as the basis for research questions. It is important to provide a degree of acceptance to all responses at this stage.

Step 3: Lists can now be classified and headings given to each group.

Step 4: Display brainstorm lists around the room. Encourage students to keep adding to or modifying lists throughout the unit.

NOTES

- Brainstorms may include words, pictures or sentences.
- Ask students to write words onto cards for ease of grouping

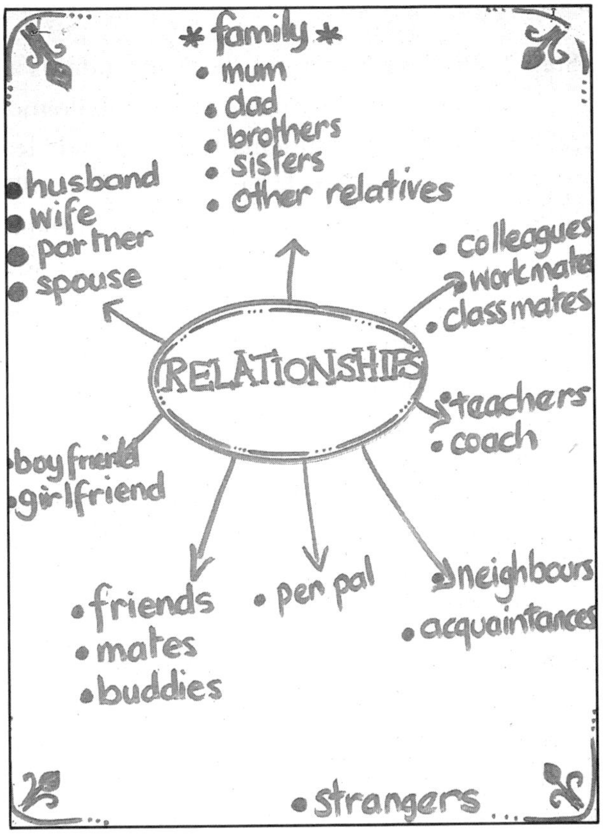

Figure 10 *A structured brainstorm about relationships*

Learning logs

PURPOSE

- to assist students to reflect on their own learning
- to provide a source of data for assessment
- to provide teachers with an insight into students' understandings and attitudes as well as their perceptions of their own strengths and weaknesses

PROCEDURE

Step 1: Begin by modelling reflective writing through a whole-class learning log. At the end of key activities in a unit, gather the class together and jointly construct an entry. Alternatively, you could begin by modelling your own entries into a learning log— 'thinking aloud' as you write.

Step 2: Provide students with a set of focus questions for their own writing after a particular activity, for example:

Write about something new that you learnt today.

How did you feel about this activity?

Write about how well you worked today. What did you do well?

What would you do differently if you were to do this again?

What questions do you have (about the topic) at the moment?

Step 3: Other structures such as concept maps, diagrams and pictures can be used to assist students in writing their learning logs, as alternative ways for them to 'sort out' or express their ideas.

Step 4: Provide written feedback to students about their entry. The learning logs can become an ongoing dialogue between teacher and student.

Step 5: Encourage students to share their learning logs with others. Peers may also provide oral or written feedback.

Step 6: As students become more comfortable and confident about writing in their learning logs, you can provide less guidance by way of focus questions and instead encourage students to respond and to express their thoughts in their learning logs in the way they feel is most appropriate.

NOTES

- There are many ways to construct and use learning logs. They may be designed specifically for the unit on which you are working or they may be a general log that can be used across the curriculum and throughout the year.

- Learning logs should encourage students to reflect both on the issues that are raised during a unit and on their learning. This reflection needs to be carefully modelled and initially supported by a structure that helps students develop their reflective skills.

Figure 11 *A 9-year-old reflects on his learning through role play*

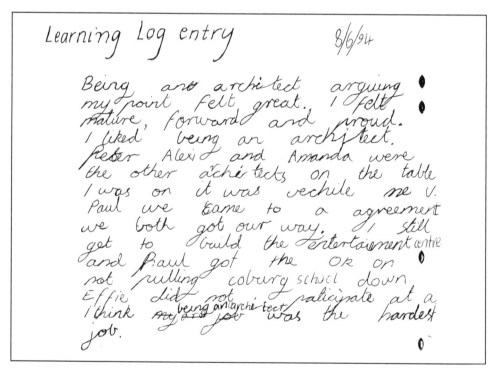

Effects wheels

PURPOSE

- to develop the understanding that events or actions have multiple consequences
- to develop students' skills at representing ideas in diagrammatic form

PROCEDURE

Step 1: Model an effects wheel with students based around a familiar topic (e.g. more homework or buying a pet). Demonstrate the ways in which each consequence leads to another.

Step 2: Select an issue or event pertinent to the topic being investigated and ask students to work individually or in pairs to construct their own effects wheel.

Step 3: Ask students to develop statements of generalisation based on the information in their effects wheel.

NOTES

• A giant effects wheel can be constructed on one wall of the classroom and added to throughout the unit.

Figure 12 *An effects wheel based on the topic of pollution*

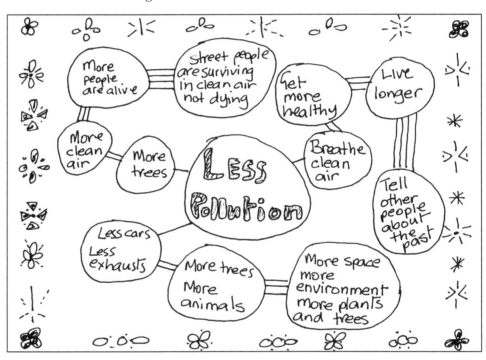

Concept maps

PURPOSE

• to help access students' prior knowledge about a topic
• to assist students to organise the ideas they have about a particular concept or topic
• to develop skills in making connections between ideas
• to provide data for assessment purposes

PROCEDURE

Step 1: Give each student approximately 10 small cards.

Step 2: On one card, they write the word/phrase that is the subject for the concept map (e.g. families).

Step 3: On the remaining cards, they write/draw other words that they consider to be important in relation to the topic.

Step 4: The cards are arranged on big sheets of paper in a way that makes sense to the student.

Step 5: Students must then show the way the ideas relate to each other by drawing lines or arrows between the related ideas. Words or connecting phrases are written on the line or arrow to make the connection clearer.

Step 6: Cards can be attached with removable adhesive to make reorganisation easier. Ask students to share maps and see if they can 'read' them.

Step 7: Generalisations can then be formed on the basis of the connecting ideas shown on the map.

NOTES

• Concept maps are useful for assessment purposes. Students could complete one at the beginning of the unit and then reconstruct it during and at the end of the unit to demonstrate their changed understandings.

• Concept maps are often best done individually, as they reflect the student's personal view of the topic.

• Pictures rather than words can be used with young students.

Figure 13 *One 8-year-old's perception of families*

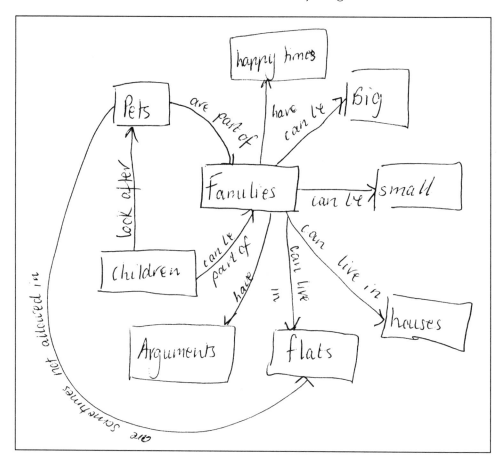

Laying it on the line

PURPOSE

- to help students to explore and clarify their own values
- to develop empathy with others
- to develop confidence in articulating and justifying opinions and beliefs
- to explore the values that underpin decision-making
- to help students recognise that people respond to issues and situations in different ways, according to the values they hold

PROCEDURE

This can be done as an oral or written activity—or the two could be combined.

Step 1: Place signs around the room (e.g. strongly agree, partially agree, partially disagree, strongly disagree). These may be placed, for example, in each corner or along a line.

Step 2: Read out a controversial statement, such as 'Men use machines more often than women' to which students must respond by placing themselves along a line or in a corner, according to the extent to which they agree/disagree with the statement.

Step 3: Once students have moved to their preferred position, conduct some 'on the spot' interviews with them, asking them to explain why they have chosen that position.

Step 4: After the activity, ask the students to comment on the way they felt about having to make decisions about where they 'stood', for example pressure to stand where their friends were, uncertainty about the topic or issue, uncertainty about their own beliefs.

Step 5: Ask students to reflect on what the activity has taught them. 'Why do we think about things so differently from one another?', 'How do our beliefs and values influence our decisions and actions?', 'How and why do our values change?'

NOTES

- Once students are familiar with the strategy, they can design their own startling statements for the activity.
- This activity may also be carried out in written form.

PNI: Positive – negative – interesting to see

PURPOSE

- to assist students to analyse a particular issue
- to encourage creative thinking
- to develop the understanding that there are many ways of looking at one issue

PROCEDURE

This activity is often most useful once students have investigated the topic for some time. They will then have information and experience to bring to the exercise

Step 1: Select an issue that is related to the topic being studied, for example 'If all world leaders were women'.

Step 2: Brainstorm the issues arising from this possibility under the three headings:

positive: focusing on perceived positive outcomes

negative: focusing on perceived negative outcomes

interesting to see: being the issues and questions that arise from the idea

NOTES

- This activity can be used as a springboard for more formalised debates or persuasive writing.

Putting you in the picture

PURPOSE

- to develop in students an understanding of the connection between themselves and the unit topic
- to encourage students to think more deeply about their own feelings, values, attitudes and actions
- to develop positive self-esteem and self-awareness
- to help students to develop a connection between their personal lives and the global domain
- to assess students' understanding of the content and relevance of the topic being studied

PROCEDURE

Step 1: Give students a simple outline of a picture frame or ask them to draw one on the page.

Step 2: Ask students to think about the topic they have been exploring and all the things they have learnt. Now ask: 'What has this got to do with you? Where do you fit into the picture?'

Step 3: Students then draw, write or map their ideas about the connections between the topic and themselves.

Step 4: Share frames with others and display them, gallery style, around the classroom.

Learning maps

PURPOSE

- to help students to develop an understanding of the purposes behind the activities in which they are engaged
- to help students to develop skills of reflection
- to gather data for evaluation purposes about successful and less successful aspects of the unit
- to assist students in understanding the process of inquiry itself
- to promote self-assessment

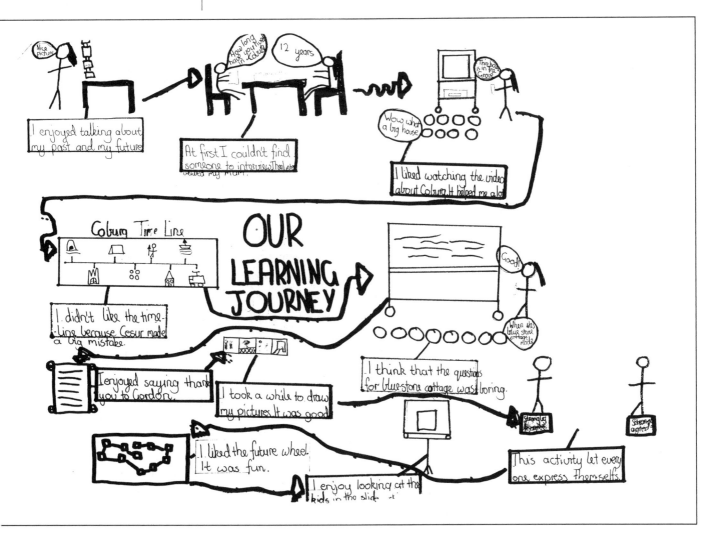

Figure 14 *A 9-year-old uses a learning map to reflect on his journey*

PROCEDURE

Step 1: Gather the class together and discuss the unit of work that has been completed. Ask students to recall the activities covered. Memories can be jogged by rereading learning logs, looking at displays around the room, etc.

Step 2: In pairs or individually, ask students to draw the journey of the unit as they might a story map. The maps should be sequential.

Step 3: Encourage students to write a brief recount (if appropriate) of the various activities in which they were involved.

Step 4 Now ask students to annotate their maps with some reflective comments about how they felt about the activities, which sections of the unit they liked the most and least, and why, etc.

Step 5: Share the maps with each other and note differences and similarities amongst the various perceptions of the unit.

NOTES

• These maps make an excellent display for parents and other members of the community to find out about the unit.

- Maps may also be made using models or through a series of small role-plays.
- Keep a photographic record of the unit and make a large class unit map with captions beneath each photo.

Expert groups

PURPOSE

- to help students to deal with a large body of information
- to encourage peer teaching
- to involve all students in gathering and disseminating information

PROCEDURE

Step 1: Organise students into small home groups. These groups discuss the topic or task at hand and delegate each member to explore an aspect of the task. For example, the topic might be 'families' and so each member is given a different aspect of family life to investigate, read about or gather information about (e.g. sources of conflict, composition, celebrations).

Step 2 Each member now moves into expert groups who share the same focus for investigation.

Step 3: Expert groups then dissolve and members return to their home groups to teach the information they have gathered to others.

NOTES

- This strategy can be used to deal with information in the space of one or two sessions or may be used to organise an investigation over a longer period of time.

Directed reading and thinking activity (DRTA)

PURPOSE

- to assist the reader to become more conscious of the text they are reading, listening to or viewing through prediction, problem-solving and questioning
- to assist the reader, listener, or viewer to become aware of the ways in which texts make meaning by focusing on the structure of the text and the language used
- to develop a critical approach to reading, listening and viewing texts through discussion of the values inherent in the text and the values that the reader, listener or viewer brings to the text

PROCEDURE

Step 1: Select a text (oral, written or visual) that deals with an issue related to the unit of work being studied.

Step 2: Students to read, hear or view the first part of the text and then stop at a designated point. Students predict what the author, speaker or character may say next and justify their predictions by referring directly to the text and what they have already read, heard or viewed.

Step 3: Designate where the text will be read to next and ask the students to stop at a particular point. Students read, hear or view the next part of the text and stop, predict and confirm what has been written, spoken or presented for viewing. This cycle is repeated about four or five times.

Step 4: Students consider the way in which the person creating the text has used language or visuals to create meaning in the text. They discuss how the language has been used to construct a particular viewpoint, reconstruct an event in history, report on a current issue, persuade an audience and so on.

Step 5: Students, with the teacher, express their feelings and opinions about the text. They may comment on the structure and language used in the text as well as on the theme or issue being raised by the text.

Step 6: Some students may be challenged to consider what they are bringing to the text in terms of their own values and experiences, and also how their life experiences influence what they take away from the text.

NOTES

- The process of reading and stopping occurs in a cycle. The final stop should be close to the end of the text.
- You could ask the students to read a written text silently, or read the text for them.
- DRTA can be extended to texts that students view, for example a film, documentary, television program, or series of advertisements in a magazine.
- DRTA should help students to develop a critical approach to reading, listening to, or viewing texts. They are supported in this by explicit reference to the ways in which the text creates meaning and discussion about the values of the creator of the text and their own value positions as readers, listeners and viewers.

Possible sentences

PURPOSE

- to enable students to bring knowledge about a particular topic or issue to predict how words in a text may be used
- to provide students with the opportunity to make predictions about the text and to confirm or reject their predictions after reading, listening to, or viewing the text
- to provide students with a support which 'tunes them in' to the text they are reading, listening to, or viewing

PROCEDURE

Step 1: Select a text (oral, written or visual) dealing with an issue related to the unit of work being studied.

Step 2: Display the title of the text and ask students to predict what they think the text might be about. They can also predict the genre of the text, for example 'A Woman of Power' could be a biography, and a documentary entitled 'Technology 2000' could be a report on technological advancements.

Step 3: Display a list of key words taken from the text and read through them. Do not provide any meanings at this stage.

Step 4: Students take the key words and put them into sentences that might provide the information contained in the text. They must use all the words from the list, and the sentences do not have to be connected. Students provide meanings for all the words, even if they are unfamiliar with the them.

Step 5: Students read the sentences to each other or to the whole class.

Step 6: Students read, listen to, or view the text and confirm, modify or reject their predictions. Any additional information provided in the text is discussed.

Step 7: Students discuss their predictions in relation to the text.

NOTES

- This strategy can be extended to texts that students view, for example a film, documentary, television program, or series of advertisements in a magazine.
- Students could reveal where their original predictions came from, the source of their knowledge and experience in the particular area of study.
- Students could illustrate their predictions.

Three level guide

PURPOSE

- to enable students to read a text at different levels to uncover the layers of meaning within the text
- to provide students with the opportunity to discuss with their peers, the meanings they have taken from the text
- to encourage students to become aware of the values they bring to the text and the influence of prior experience on their reading of the text
- to allow students the opportunity to add to, refine, or modify the meanings they have taken from the text

PROCEDURE

Step 1: Select a text (oral, written or visual) that deals with an issue related to the unit of work being studied.

Step 2: Design statements about the text based on three levels of understanding. Students must indicate 'true' or 'false' in response

　　1 Literal: statements related directly to the text, e.g. 'Vietnam is located in South-East Asia.'

　　2 Interpretive: statements that require the student to interpret

information, e.g. 'The United States exerted its power over Vietnam after the war.'

3 Analytical: statements that require students to look at the big picture'—the broader issues in relation to the text—e.g. 'Trade embargoes should not be used under any circumstances.'

NOTES

- Students work through the task individually then share in groups.
- The sharing enables them to discuss, challenge, modify, reject and confirm responses.
- Responses to the second and third groups of statements may involve students in lengthy discussions which could involve returning to the text to substantiate their viewpoint.

Moral dilemmas

PURPOSE

- to allow students to look at a particular issue from a range of viewpoints
- to develop a respect for different viewpoints
- to expose students to a hypothetical situation which provides for the clarification of their own values and identification of the value positions of others

PROCEDURE

Step 1: Select a text (oral, written or visual) that deals with an issue related to the unit of work being studied. The text should contain a hypothetical situation in which the central character is faced with two choices, for example: 'A central character finds a large sum of money and must decide whether to report it to the police or use it to buy medicine for his/her sick mother.' The choices must be feasible and produce a mental conflict or dilemma.

Step 2: Students read, listen to, or view the text and discuss the choices that the character is faced with. This discussion may require simple guidance, for example:

What could ... do?

What should ... do?

List the consequences of each decision.

List all the possible choices that ... could make. Choose the one you think is the best choice.

List all the possible choices that ... could make. Place these in order from best option to least best option.

Step 3: Students discuss the options they have considered and share with the whole class.

NOTES

- Moral dilemmas can be very simple at first and then become more complicated as additional factors are presented.

• This strategy could also be presented using a moral biography approach. The story of a person's life is outlined for the students and they consider the choices that were or could possibly be presented to the person and consider the consequences of these choices. For example, the students could study the life story of Nelson Mandela and consider the options he had in his fight for equality for black Africans.

Concept attainment

PURPOSE

• to provide students with the opportunity to develop their understandings of new concepts
• to provide students with the opportunity to make links between new concepts

PROCEDURES

Step 1: Without telling students, decide on a concept to be introduced, modified or expanded upon, for example 'government', 'family', 'trade'.

Step 2 Draw a simple 'Yes/No' table on the chalkboard.

Step 3: Provide the students with an example(s) of words associated with the chosen concept. For example, words such as *horse and carriage, kerosene,* and *washboard* could be associated with the concept of 'life in the past'.

Step 4: Ask the students to guess the concept by suggesting their own words. If their guesses are associated with the concept, they are placed in the 'Yes' column, if not they are placed in the 'No' column. This step is repeated until the concept is attained.

NOTES

• Concepts generated can be used to develop generalisations about the topic, or issue being studied.
• Concepts generated can be used as the basis for written or oral language activities.

Grouping strategies

PURPOSE

• to develop students' skills in working cooperatively with others
• to foster a willingness to work with different people at different times
• to develop tolerance, adaptability and appreciation of the contributions others make to a given task

PROCEDURES

Friendship grouping

This is often the most common form of grouping in the classroom but can be the least effective. Nevertheless, it is important that opportunities are given to students to select their own groups at times and this will often result in friendship-based groups. It may be useful to say to students 'When organising your group, think about those people with whom you would work most effectively and efficiently.' Ask students to reflect on the success of their selected groupings after they have completed the task.

Random grouping

Random groups can be a more equitable way of organising students for cooperative activities, and there are many ways in which they can be achieved. The following gimmicks can help vary the ways in which random groups are formed and bring an element of fun into the procedure:

- Names out of a hat: Place all students' names in a hat and simply pick them out to form random groups. Gender balance can be achieved by placing names on different colored paper or by alternating between two hats.
- Birthdays: Group students according to birthday months or dates. Some shuffling may need to be done to achieve final numbers.
- Matching up: Give students each a card with a number on it. They must then make groups such as multiples of 2, or numbers that add up to 20. A similar activity can be done with words. Give students one half each of compound words; they must find their partner. Pairs then join to make groups of four or six.
- Silent color match: Place a colored star or sticker on each child's forehead or back (somewhere where they can't see it). The colors can be selected according to the size and number of groups required. In silence, students must organise themselves into groups that share the same color. This strategy has the added bonus of requiring students to help one another!
- Parts of the whole: This strategy can be linked well with the current topic you are studying. Again, students are given a label they cannot see. The word or picture belongs with others that, when together, make up a whole item. For example, it may be buildings in a school, parts of the body or states in a country. In silence, students must find the other words or pictures that belong with them. The combination of people becomes the group.

Needs-based or interest-based groups

Groups may also be formed on the basis of particular needs or interests shared by several students. It is important for students to understand that there are times when the teacher will determine the structure of the groups—just as there are times when they will be random or self-selected. Some students may benefit from being grouped with others who need more assistance with a task and will therefore work intensively with the teacher. Others may be grouped in order to challenge and extend. Needs-based grouping should be used selectively.

Multi-age/multi-ability groups

Random grouping will often result in a mixed ability arrangement but it may be more specifically designed for this purpose. Mixed ability groupings provide an excellent opportunity for students to learn from one another. Students become important models to each other and also benefit from the opportunity to help and support each other.

NOTES

- While cooperative groups are an essential part of effective teaching and learning in social education, students should also have opportunities to work individually or as a class.
- Aim towards using a balance of grouping strategies over a unit.

Figure 15 *Rules for working cooperatively*

CHAPTER 4

Over to you

PLANNING YOUR OWN UNITS OF WORK

The units in this book serve not only as a resource for teaching but also as models for planning your own units of work for social education. Once you have worked with some of these units, the overall sequence of activities will become familiar and will enable you to begin developing units around other topics.

The planning sequence we have used should be seen as a guide rather than a recipe. The theory of an inquiry-based, integrated curriculum (as outlined in chapter 1) provides a conceptual framework within which to develop and modify units according to the particular topic you have selected, the context in which you teach and, of course, the students you are teaching.

For some teachers, the planning of a unit of work will not be new. We hope this chapter will provide you with ideas that help refine or add to your existing repertoire. For those for whom unit planning is a relatively new experience, the following advice is offered:

Plan ahead. Unit topics should be mapped out across the year. Balance units developed for social education with those that focus more on the environment, others that are grounded in physical science and others in the health area. Consider special events in the year (e.g. school camp, Easter, book week) and decide whether you will treat these within the context of a unit, as a separate and short mini-unit or not at all. Every special event does not need to be dealt with every year!

Plan in teams. The best units of work we have seen in action are those to which a group of teachers have made a contribution. Team planning enriches the scope of a unit and reduces the workload for the individual. It also allows a basis for discussion, group evaluation and monitoring of the unit. Teams do not necessarily need to be made up of teachers working with the same year level and will benefit from including specialist teachers such as librarians and art teachers.

Set aside a sustained block of time for planning. Some schools have introduced a planning day each term when teachers are released to work together on unit planning. Whilst the planning task may seem lengthy in the early stages, the workload is reduced on a week-to-week basis because a long-term picture of the unit has been developed.

Keep clear, written documentation of units and make these available for other staff to share. A space in the library or staff room may be allocated to store copies of units. Agree on a basic format to develop a consistent approach to planning and documenting across the school.

Discuss unit topics at a whole-school level and purchase resources for the school with these topics in mind. Some schools organise unit boxes or kits that teachers can borrow to help streamline the planning process. These can be added to as units are taught and more resources are discovered.

Maintain an open door policy in the school and encourage staff to visit other classrooms. Strategies for social education can be adapted across the school—something seen in a year 1 room may trigger an idea for the year 6 teacher and so on. This is also a useful way of encouraging people to be constructively critical of their own and others' practice.

Consider the relationship between language and social education. Plan for an explicit focus on a written/spoken genre. Choose texts (written, spoken, visual) to complement the unit of work and plan activities which allow students to explore the meanings they bring to and take from the text.

The following blackline masters are designed to assist you with your own unit planning and evaluation. Good luck!

CHECKLIST FOR UNIT PLANNING

The following questions provide a useful checklist to run through during the planning process.

When planning a unit, ask yourself:

- What do I/we **know** about this topic? How do I **feel** about it? What do I need to know? How is this influencing my planning and selection of resources?
- Is the topic **relevant and appropriate** to this group of students (their age, lives, needs, experiences, community)?
- Does the topic develop some of the **'big ideas'** about the social world and does it link to the perspectives in social education?
- Have I provided experiences through which students will **inquire and discover things for themselves**? Will they investigate the topic in a range of ways (reading, surveys, interviewing, observing)?
- Have I provided opportunities for students to explore the **values and attitudes** associated with this topic?
- Does the unit allow **cooperative learning, problem-solving, and active decision-making** to take place?
- Does the unit draw on a **range of curriculum areas** in purposeful ways?
- Are teaching strategies and content within the unit in keeping with **social justice, ecological sustainability** and **democratic processes**?
- Have I considered the various opportunities for **language development** in this unit? What use of texts does the content best lend itself to?
- Is there potential for an **action** component in this unit? Have I allowed opportunities for students to act upon what they have learnt?
- Can this topic help **make a difference** to the lives of my students?
- Have I provided opportunities for students to **reflect** on their learning throughout the unit?
- Have I provided opportunities for the students to *critically engage* with the texts used in the unit?

SKILLS FOR SOCIAL EDUCATION

The following table summarises some of the key skills students use in social education and can be used as a basis for your planning, evaluation or assessment of student learning. Skills can be checked off at the end of each unit using a coding system to identify those covered (e.g. skills covered in Focus on Families could be identified by a red tick, those covered in 'Trading Places' could be identified by a blue tick, and so on). This will help you to identify the 'gaps' in your planning or in students' experiences, and prompt the planning of appropriate activities in the units that follow.

Gathering and recording information

interviewing ☐
observing ☐
designing and conducting questionnaires ☐
reading text (fiction, non-fiction) ☐
discussing ☐
reading pictures, maps and graphs ☐
taking notes ☐
listening predicting ☐
brainstorming ☐
viewing ☐
predicting ☐
forming questions ☐

Skills for communicating with others

presenting orally ☐
discussing ☐
listening ☐
writing in a range of genre (reports, explanation, procedures, persuasive, recount, narrative, etc.) ☐
role-play ☐
debating ☐
mapping ☐
graphing ☐
illustrating ☐
performing ☐
writing ☐
improvising ☐
story telling ☐
using non-verbal means (dance, mime etc.) ☐

Making sense of information

writing ☐
summarising ☐
speaking ☐
sorting and sequencing—timelines, flowcharts, etc. ☐
analysing ☐
discussing ☐
categorising ☐
choosing ☐
restating ☐
reading graphs and tables ☐
reading maps ☐
creating key visuals ☐
statistical analysis ☐
comparing and contrasting ☐
confirming ☐
modifying ☐
rejecting ☐
critical reading of texts ☐
recalling and recounting ☐
improvising ☐

Skills for working with others

working with partners ☐
working in cooperative groups ☐
reaching consensus ☐
compromising ☐
listening ☐
speaking ☐
tolerating the views of others ☐
challenging justifying ☐
criticising ideas, not people ☐
giving and receiving feedback
delegating and accepting responsibilities ☐
sharing ☐

Skills for examining beliefs, opinions and values

identifying ☐
clarifying ☐
role-play ☐
ranking and prioritising ☐
choosing ☐
justifying ☐
supposing ☐
debating ☐
showing evidence ☐
writing ☐
speaking ☐
listening ☐
achieving consensus ☐
empathising ☐
responding ☐
stating an opinion ☐
expressing an opinion ☐

Skills for reflecting and acting on information

reflecting (e.g. reflective writing) ☐
evaluating ☐
self-assessing ☐
predicting and confirming ☐
concept mapping ☐
debating ☐
planning ☐
presenting a point of view ☐
developing alternatives ☐
working within a time limit ☐
generalising ☐
decision-making ☐
solving problems ☐

STRATEGY AUDIT

This table will help you to keep a record of strategies used in your own units and is also a useful reminder of some of the strategies available to you. Add your own strategies.

Strategy	Unit	Unit	Unit	Unit	Unit	Unit	Unit
Concept maps							
Concept attainment							
Consensus 1-3-6							
Conversation counters							
De Bono's 6 thinking hats							
DRTA							
Effects wheels							
Expert groups							
Grouping strategies							
Interviews and surveys							
Laying it on the line							
Learning logs							
Learning maps							
Moral dilemmas							
People bingo							
PNI							
Possible sentences							
Putting you in the picture							
Research contracts							
Structured brainstorm							
Three level guide							
Watch this space							

SAMPLE PLANNER

Topic: **Year level/group:** **Understandings:** **Key perspectives:** **Outcomes:**

Inquiry sequence	Use of texts/ resources	Language focus	Activity sequence	Language focus	Key skills	Key strategies	Outcomes	Notes
Tuning in Sensitising and motivating students								
Preparing to find out Seeking prior knowledge, focusing on what students might find out and experience in stages to follow								
Finding out Shared experiences to gather new information								
Sorting out Using a range of areas (art, maths, drama, language, movement, music, etc.) to process information that has been gathered Going further								
Challenging and extending students								
Making connections Drawing conclusions, reflecting on learning								
Taking action Applying learning to everyday life								

UNIT 1

LOOKING BACK

A unit about local history and change, for middle to upper primary students

ABOUT THIS UNIT

This unit focuses on the history of the local area in which students attend school, which may also be the area where many of them live. It is designed to develop a broad understanding of the nature of change and to explore some of the complex tensions that exist between change and stability, progress and conservation, and tradition and innovation. Through listening to the oral histories of older people, students are encouraged not only to appreciate the 'authority of experience' but also to question the meanings behind such stories and accounts. The unit also offers an interesting opportunity to examine the way the same event can be seen from a range of perspectives.

45

During the unit, students are encouraged to consider their own values in relation to change; to compare values across generations; and to question or justify their own values. Parents and, in particular, grandparents or older members of the community can be effectively involved.

KEY TERMS

history	generation
community	memorabilia
environment	indigenous/non-indigenous
heritage	

UNDERSTANDINGS AROUND WHICH THE UNIT IS BASED

People and places are in a constant state of change.

People respond to changes in their immediate environment in different ways.

Changes in the past can often provide people with ideas about how things might change in the future.

Our neighborhood has features that make it unique.

Conservation measures can be applied to both the natural and the built environment. Some buildings are protected by the special organisations.

People value their local environment in different ways.

KEY PERSPECTIVES IN SOCIAL EDUCATION

Imagining and constructing the future

Thinking critically

Living with uncertainty

Cultural heritage

Changing lifestyles

Developing values

KEY LEARNING OUTCOMES FOR SOCIAL EDUCATION

Identifies similarities and differences in the lives of different generations

Describes different periods of time in the local area

Critically interprets accounts and artefacts from other times

Sequences a set of events in chronological order

Identifies, reflects on and analyses aspects of environments and family ways of life that have endured or changed

Proposes reasons as to why the local community and environment have changed or are likely to change

Portrays an event or occasion from a different perspective

Describes places according to their natural and built features

Locates familiar places on maps of both past and present localities

Explores and clarifies values behind the choices people make in their use of places

Describes different views of individuals and groups about issues related to the care of places

Considers own place within the current and future community

Reflects on the consequences of decisions made in a life and the extent to which we can or cannot shape our future

LANGUAGE OUTCOMES

Uses written and oral language for recounting an event or experience

Demonstrates an understanding of the role of oral language in sustaining culture

Listens to and records other people's ideas and experiences

Interprets and communicates other people's ideas and experiences

Provides examples of ways in which written and oral language have changed over time

Analyses and interprets texts from a range of perspectives

SELECTION OF TEXTS

You will need to consider the range of texts (written, spoken and visual) needed to help students access information about the history of the local area. Texts could include maps, diary entries, oral histories, discussions with guest speakers, written recounts, photographs and so on.

DEVELOPING A CRITICAL PERSPECTIVE

As students will be using a wide range of texts, it is essential that they consider the authenticity of these texts and the reliability of the data and so read the texts with a critical perspective. This is particularly important given that history is the recounting of events, involving people and places, and is open to differing interpretations. Attention should be given to the ways in which a given event may be recounted differently according to the person creating it.

Focus on genre: recount

This unit requires students to develop understandings about local history, and therefore lends itself well to the explicit teaching of the recount genre (factual, personal and imaginative). Students use recounts for accessing information and experience, and as models for the creation of written and oral recounts to process their understandings. Explicit teaching of this genre provides students with greater control over it and will add to their repertoire of oral and written language skills. This focus on genre is a 'unit within a unit' and we suggest you take time to focus on the modelling and application of the genre.

Note that the unit allows for the exploration of all three types of recount: personal (such as a diary), factual (such as a newspaper report), and imaginative (such as a fictional account of life 100 years ago). The structure remains essentially the same, although these types of recount differ minimally in the type of language used.

KEY FEATURES OF THE RECOUNT GENRE

Purpose: A recount reconstructs events or an experience.

Structure: A recount begins with an **orientation**, for example:

Mary Brown has lived in Greenhills since 1905

and this is followed by a series of **events**:

Mary went to school at Greenhills State School and was one of the first women to be accepted into Brown State University.

Language used: Usually the participants in a recount are specific as in this example with *Mary Brown*. The simple tense is used (*Mary Brown studied*) and there is the use of action verbs such as *lived, moved, married*. There are linking words to do with time (*then, after that, next, before*). In personal recounts, personal pronouns such as *I* and *we* are used; in factual recounts such as historical recounts the third person is used; and an imaginative recount usually uses the first person.

TEACHING SEQUENCE: RECOUNTS

The following shows *one approach* to teaching key features of the information genre. For more detailed advice refer to Derewianka (1990) and Wing Jan (1991).

Teacher modelling: A range of models of recounts (written and oral) can be used. For this unit in particular, recounts depicting the life of a person who lived in the local area, a reconstruction of an event, for example preparing for a wedding, or an imaginative recount of what life one hundred years ago may have been like could be used. These recounts allow students to access information, and also work as models for their own writing or oral recount. You could create your own personal, factual or imaginative recount to model and demonstrate the key features of the genre to your students.

Spotlight on structure: The structure of a recount relates to the purpose of the text and its intended audience. Questioning students about the structure of the text allows them to focus on the particular structure of this genre and apply this to their own writing or oral language.

How is the written/oral recount structured?

Is there an orientation?

Is the orientation followed by a series of events?

Spotlight on language features: Language used in a recount helps to create the particular meaning of the text. A focus on how the language is used to create meaning enables students to choose the language appropriate to this genre in their own writing or oral language.

What pronouns have been used?

Are there any action verbs?

Have linking words to do with time been included?

Other things to consider:

Have you been able to locate accurate information?

Have you been able to include information relevant to your audience?
Will your audience understand your information?
Is your information accurate?
Have you included the most important facts and information?

PREPARATION

- Organise learning logs for each child (see chapter 3).
- Contact local historical society/local council—find out whether any videos or picture sets have been compiled showing changes to the local area.
- Consider guest speakers—people who have lived in the area for a long time.
- Collect artefacts that could be used throughout the unit, e.g. old phtographs, memorabilia, maps, etc.

TUNING IN: SAMPLE ACTIVITIES

PURPOSE

- to provide students with opportunities to become engaged with the topic
- to ascertain the students' initial curiosity about the topic
- to allow students to share their personal experience of the topic

1 Personal histories

Students consider five important events in their own lives so far. (This could be triggered by sharing five significant events in your own life.) Each event is drawn and/or written about on a card and placed in chronological order on their table. Students then move around the room and examine each other's accounts. Ask:

What patterns do you notice?
What things do people consider to be significant moments in their lives?
What have been the consequences of some of these events in your life?

Introduce the concept of a personal history.

2 Word association

Ask students to write or draw anything that comes to mind when they hear the word *history*. Develop a working definition of the word that can be refined throughout the unit.

3 Memorabilia

Encourage students to begin asking their parents, neighbors or friends about their recollection of their local area as it was many years ago. Invite them to bring in old photographs and items of memorabilia.

4 A few of my favorite things

With parents' permission, students bring to school mething that is very special to them. When sharing these with the class, they must explain why that item is so important to them. Discuss the fact that they each value different things but often for the same reasons. Discuss items that students may have kept over many years for sentimental reasons, for example a teddy bear they had as a baby or a special piece of jewellery. Why are these things so precious?

Figure 16 *Students compile
personal histories which are
then displayed for sharing*

5 Special memories

Ask students to write about a particular vivid memory they have—it may be their earliest conscious memory. Share these special memories as an introduction to the language of oral history. Introduce the notion that our memories may often embellish or change the nature of the event. Students may then ask their parents/grandparents about a special memory and compare the way each tells the same story.

PREPARING TO FIND OUT: SAMPLE ACTIVITIES

PURPOSE

- to find out what the students already know about the topic
- to provide the students with a focus for the forthcoming experience
- to help in the planning of further experience and activities

6 Listing and bundling

In small groups, students brainstorm as many places that they can think of that exist in their neighborhood. These lists are then grouped and labelled, for example:

  shops
  factories
  entertainment
  sports venues
  schools
  parks

Figure 17 *The list is displayed and added to during the unit.*

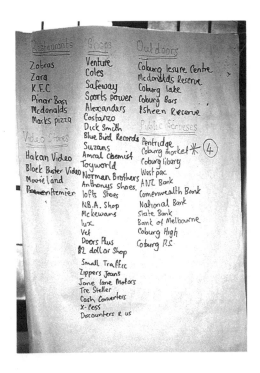

7 Imagining the past

From the lists that have been created in activity 6, students select one place to focus on. Their task is to imagine what this place might have looked like many many years ago (set the time frame relevant to the students or to the area itself, e.g. 100 years ago). They then represent the place as it is now and as they think it might have been back then. Display and discuss the representations, for example:

> *What do your pictures tell us about the way we imagine the past might have been like?*
> *What things have many people included in their pictures? Why?*
> *Are there any representations that you should challenge or question?*
> *What questions do these pictures make you want to ask?*
> *Why do you think you have created these images. Where do you think you have got your ideas from?*
> *What other images might have influenced you?*

Retain the pictures for use later on in the unit when students will return to add a third picture of their image of the place in the future.

8 Questions

Begin a list of questions about the history of the local area. The list can be added to over the course of the unit.

9 Statements: What do we know?

Students have been asked to gather some initial information about the history of the area from friends and family. Individually, they write down two statements summarising what they have found out. They need to check their statements with someone else before writing them onto a paper strip. Strips are then displayed and organised into groups. Note any questions that arise and add to the list.

10 Through the window

Share with students a picture book that shows the way in which a place has changed over time. One example is *Window* by Jeannie Baker. As the illustrations are very detailed, it would be best to have multiple copies of this book available. Give five focus groups a different aspect to look for as they view the pages:

1. Housing: *How did people's housing change over time?*

2. Vegetation: *How did the vegetation change over time?*
3. Animals: *What kinds of animals do you see in the pictures and how do they change?*
4. Transport: *What methods of transport do people use? How do these change over time?*
5. Lifestyle: *What sorts of things are people doing in each picture? How do their activities change over time?*

Groups then meet to discuss and record their observations. Using the 'expert groups' strategy (see chapter 3), groups disperse and share their ideas with others. Ideas can be recorded on charts to summarise key changes that took place over time. Ask:

What are some of the things that you think might have caused these changes to take place?

What images about change was the author trying to convey?

11 How can we find out?

Make a class list of strategies for finding out about the history of the local area. Ask students:

How can we find out more about the way our local area used to be, and how and why it has changed over time?

FINDING OUT: SAMPLE ACTIVITIES

PURPOSE

- to further stimulate the students' curiosity
- to provide new information which may answer some of the students' earlier questions
- to raise other questions for the students to explore in the future
- to challenge the students' knowledge, beliefs and values
- to help students make sense of further activities and experiences which have been planned for them

12 Mapping our place

This activity is designed to help develop students' familiarity with their local area. The result—a giant map—can be quite spectacular and provides a key reference for activities throughout the unit. This is particularly helpful for students who do not live close to the school or are new to the area. (See figure 19 for an example.)

Provide each student with a copy of a map of the local area, including the school. (You may wish to conduct a few mapping and location activities to help students 'read' the map.) The size of the area you include will depend on the nature of the area and the extent to which you would like to develop this particular task. Divide the class into pairs or trios and assign each group a section of the map. Their task is to visit that particular area at some stage over the next week or two. Later in the unit, students will join their section of the map with others—thus creating a large map of the area.

13 Tell me a story

Some of the most valuable information about local history can be gathered from older people who have lived in the place for many years and have seen changes taking place. Individually or in pairs, students interview an older person about their memories of the local area. Questions should be devised by the whole class and used as the basis for each interview, although they will need to be modified from person to person.

Run some mock interviews in preparation for the data-gathering exercise. Focus on interview protocol: showing the person that you are listening and interested in what they have to say, asking permission to tape the interview, thanking them at the end of the interview, etc. Encourage students to record the interview in some way—audio, video or written records would all be appropriate.

14 Guest speaker

Invite a local historian to discuss the history of the local area and, hopefully, bring in some 'artefacts' to share. Prepare a list of questions beforehand.

Perhaps the guest could lead the class on a local walk.

15 Excursion

Visit a site of some historical significance, such as an old home, a piece of land or area significant to people indigenous to the area, or an early structure such as a bridge or clock tower. Walk around the local area to identify periods of time in which certain parts were built. For example, identify 'old' and 'new' houses, parks that have been recently made, etc.

16 Visual texts

Local historical societies sometimes have slides, films, or videos outlining aspects of local history. It may be possible to view a map of the area drawn from the perspective of indigenous people, showing different names for places and perhaps different boundaries. When examining visual images such as these, ask students to consider:

Whose 'version' of history is being shown here?

How might, for example, indigenous people of the area have created a different image?

SORTING OUT: SAMPLE ACTIVITIES

PURPOSE

- to provide students with concrete means of sorting out and representing information and ideas arising from the 'finding out' stage
- to provide students with the opportunity to process the information they have gathered and present this in a number of ways
- to allow for a diverse range of outcomes

17 Map making

Using the information gathered in activity 12, students create a giant map of the local area based on the observations they have carried out of a particular section of the local area. This can be outlined on a large sheet of paper pinned to the wall using an overhead projection of a road map. Individually or in pairs, students work on the area of the map that they investigated. Provide them with a range of materials that could be used to represent their ideas: some useful materials are fabric and fabric glue; paint; matchboxes; sequins; colored paper; wool.

Label key areas of the map and add information to it as the unit progresses. Significant historical sites could be highlighted.

18 Timelines

As key dates and events are gathered during the 'finding out' stage, students place these on a timeline showing, to scale, the intervals between these key dates. Of particular importance to this activity is the recognition of time prior to the arrival of non-indigenous people to the area.

Figure 19 *The map forms a key reference for activities throughout the unit*

19 Working with data gathered from interviews

Tapes and transcripts of interviews should be shared throughout the unit, thereby drawing common threads together. A number of strategies can be used to help students make sense of the information they have gathered from older people. Some suggestions are:

- Select a key excerpt from an oral history and dramatise the event to the rest of the class.
- Prepare a 'personal history' similar to the ones made in activity 1. This time the significant moments are drawn from the person interviewed.
- Prepare a report of the interview to include in the school newsletter.
- Write a letter of thanks to the person interviewed.
- Set up mock interviews in pairs where one student takes on the role of the person they have interviewed and the other asks questions. The interview is re-enacted for the class.
- Compile a book of recollections based on the information gathered by the class.

As interviews are being processed, it is important to make explicit the fact that the stories have been told from one person's perspective. History is ultimately an interpretation of events by others and accounts of such events change over time as they are passed from generation to generation and retold by different people in different ways. This understanding can be drawn out by engaging students in a simple game of 'pass the message'. Seat students in a circle and whisper a message to one who then passes it on to the next and so on. The message will inevitably change by the time it has completed the circle. Ask: *How is history like a game of pass the message?*

It may be possible to find examples of ways in which the same event is told differently by the people interviewed in the local community. Of particular relevance to this concept are the interpretations often placed on the 'settlement' of a place by a new group of people. For example, many people may regard the arrival of new settlers as an invasion—a time of 'unsettlement' and destruction for indigenous people. Some records of history, however, portray these periods as a pioneering time, one of settlement and new beginnings. Investigate key events in the history of your local area. Ask: *Would everyone have viewed this in the same way?*

GOING FURTHER: SAMPLE ACTIVITIES

PURPOSE

- to extend and challenge students' understanding about the topic
- to provide for more information in order to broaden the range of understandings available to the students

20 Home of the heart

The newspaper article featured in **blackline master 5** recounts the story of an elderly resident who recounts his childhood memories of the local neighborhood. This can be used in a variety of ways, for example:

- List all the changes that have taken place over Joe's lifetime. Compare these to the kinds of changes that were noted by people that students interviewed.
- Discuss the similarities and differences between Joe's childhood and the students' own lifestyles.
- Rewrite the account from the perspective of Joe's son or wife or parents-in-law.
- Discuss students' opinions about the quality of Joe's life as he grew up in the early days of Coburg. What were some of the things they consider to be disadvantages of this time? What things do they regard positively?
- Students write a similar account of their own lives, imagining that they are 92 years old. What changes might they experience?

21 My place

Find a book that depicts social and physical changes over time. One example of this is Nadia Wheatley's book *My Place* which provides a written and visual account of the changes that have taken place in one neighborhood over 200 years. Use the book as a model to encourage students to write about the history of their own 'places', developed around their house, street or a particular building in the local community.

22 Guest speaker: a town planner

Invite a local town planner to discuss decisions that have been made in the design of the local area. Ask about current and future planning projects. Focus on the factors that have to be taken into account when planning a neighborhood.

23 Our heritage

Students could explore the notion of heritage in relation to the history of their particular area. Set up a heritage display based on the information that has been gathered in the unit. Groups of students could be assigned different aspects of heritage:

• Natural places: key places in the environment that have not been made by humans e.g. special trees, wetlands, etc.
• Cultural places: key buildings and places in the area
• Folklore: stories, songs, games linked with the local area
• Moveable objects: items gathered from the past

Set the classroom up as a museum, with captions for each item, map etc. Invite other classes and conduct tours.

24 Heritage haggling

Figure 20 *Students reflect on their role-play of a real-life issue*

Blackline master 6 outlines a scenario about a historic theatre that may be

going to be demolished to make way for an entertainment complex. This could be used as the basis of a role-play, using *blackline master 7*, to explore some of the complex issues that arise when change takes place in a local community. The scenario could be used as it is, or as a model for one based on a 'real-life' issue in the local community (e.g. trees being felled to make way for a race track, a school being closed and the land sold to a nearby shopping complex, a community through which a freeway is being built). Scan local papers for relevant events. After moving through the role-play process, ask students to reflect on the experience. Key questions to assist in debriefing may include:

Did your personal feelings about the issue conflict with the feelings of your character? How did you cope with that?

What values did the characters in your group hold most strongly?

Who did you come into conflict with? Why? How did you attempt to resolve problems?

Does this issue remind you of similar events in this community or in other parts of the country/world?

Why do people feel so differently about change?

Who 'owns' a community? Who makes the decisions? How can we influence decisions being made?

25 Cemetery visit

A visit to the local cemetery can provide many interesting classes about the history of the area and the people who once lived in it. Note the dates on headstones, showing when people were born and died, causes of death, sizes of families and the range of ways people marked the passing of their loved ones.

26 Another place

Find out about the history of another place and compare it with the area that has been studied. This might be done through literature, video or letter writing to others. Focus on the similarities in the kinds of changes that have taken place.

MAKING CONNECTIONS: SAMPLE ACTIVITIES

PURPOSE

• to help students draw conclusions about what they have learnt

27 Thinking hats

Use De Bono's thinking hats (see chapter 3) to summarise and analyse information gathered over the unit. Divide students into five groups, giving each one of the interactions below. You may wish to tailor the instructions to suit your particular area or to establish a more concrete time frame.

Black hat: Make a list of all the things you consider to have been the disadvantages of living here 100 years ago.

Yellow hat: Make a list of all the things you consider to have been positive about living here 100 years ago.

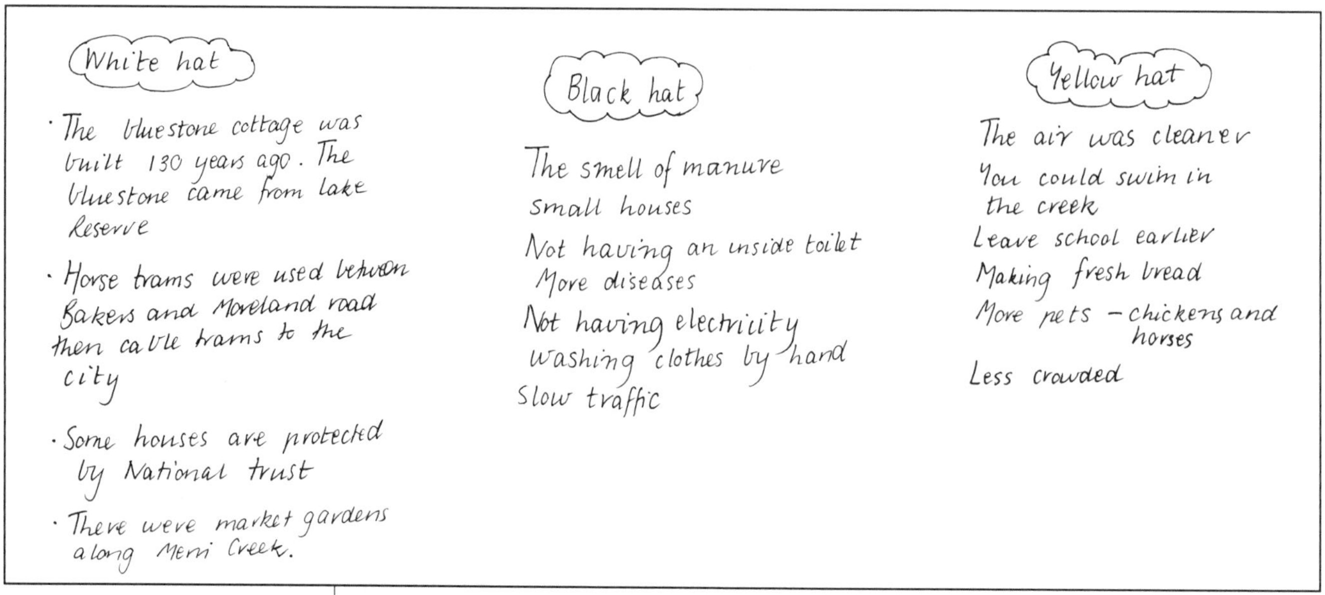

Figure 21 *Students use De Bono's thinking hats to summarise and analyse information gathered over the unit*

White hat

- The bluestone cottage was built 130 years ago. The bluestone came from lake Reserve
- Horse trams were used between Bakers and Moreland road then cable trams to the city
- Some houses are protected by National Trust
- There were market gardens along Merri Creek.

Black hat

The smell of manure
small houses
Not having an inside toilet
More diseases
Not having electricity
Washing clothes by hand
Slow traffic

Yellow hat

The air was cleaner
You could swim in the creek
Leave school earlier
Making fresh bread
More pets — chickens and horses
Less crowded

White hat: Make a list of all the facts (things that you believe are true) about life in this area 100 years ago.

Green hat: What were some of the problems that people faced living in this area 100 years ago? How did they solve their problems?

Blue hat: What kinds of changes do you imagine will occur in this area over the next 100 years? Why?

28 Data chart

Summarise the information gathered about the history of the local area onto a large data chart. Horizontal headings could include: present, future, reasons for change; vertical categories might include vegetation, lifestyle, buildings, transport. After the data chart has been completed, ask students to identify some of the key patterns they notice in the final column on 'reasons for change'.

Compile a list of factors that bring about change, and develop these into statements of generalisation.

Figure 22 *A history data chart*

29 Effects wheel

Individually, students brainstorm various ways in which they believe their local area will change in the future, based on the things they have discovered about its history, for example:

> more elderly people
>
> more roads
>
> fewer schools
>
> more supermarkets
>
> railway stations closed

Each student then selects one change around which to base an effects wheel. Here they must consider the various consequences of this change.

Once wheels have been completed and displayed, ask:

How do you feel about these possible changes?

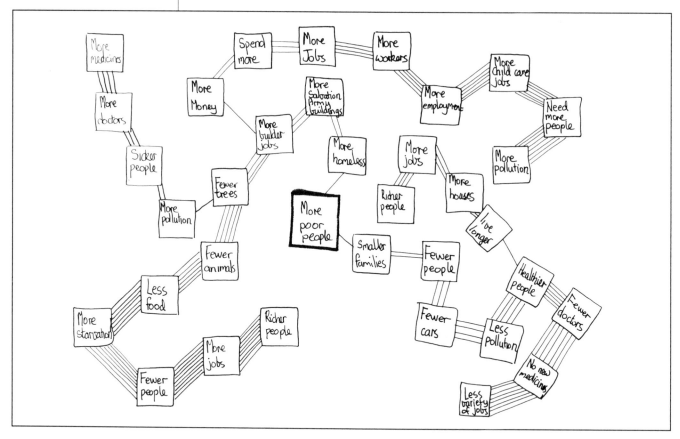

Figure 23 *An imaginative recount based on information gathered during the unit*

Can we control what happens in the future?
How are decisions made?

30 Putting you in the picture

Provide students with a simple outline of a picture frame (see chapter 3). Ask them to consider all the things they have learnt about the history of their local area and about change. Pose the questions:

How do you fit into all of this?
What has this made you think about your life?

They respond to these questions by writing or drawing an image or diagram inside the frame and then share these with others.

31 Imaginative recounts

Students now use the information they have gathered over the course of the unit to write a recount of a real or imagined event from the perspective of someone living in the past. Through the setting, descriptions of characters, use of language etc. the piece should demonstrate students' understandings of both the content of the unit and the structure of an imaginative recount.

32 Looking forward

Return to drawings made of places in the past and present from activity 7. Add a third drawing to the scene, showing an image of the place as it might look in the future.

TAKING ACTION: SAMPLE ACTIVITIES

PURPOSE

- to assist students to make links between their understandings and their experience in the real world
- to enable students to make choices and develop the belief that they can be effective participants in society
- to provide further insight into students' understandings for future unit planning

33 Heritage trail

Design a heritage trail around the local area. Students could take responsibility for the area they focused on in the map-making activity. They now set up a guided trail through that area. Brochures can be made for the trail which provide a map of the route that should be taken and a description of particular places of interest along the way. Items to include in the heritage trail might be:

old buildings
homes that have been in the area for many years
factories
churches
schools
post office
old shops
railway stations
parks
wetlands
sculptures, statues, art works

Students lead another class along their trail.

34 Grandparents' day

Students invite their grandparents or elderly friends to the school, presenting the work they have done during the unit.

35 Promote the town

Students design posters or a video that is designed to inform others about the special features of the local area.

36 Time capsules

Ask students to consider the next generation of students. What could they tell them or leave for them that would best describe our community as it is now. They prepare a time capsule to bury somewhere in the schoolgrounds.

37 Audio books

Students make their own 'audio books' to share with others. They tape their own oral histories (and may include their anticipated futures) and support and accompany the tape with texts, memorabilia, photos, etc.

Home of the heart

by Kim Behringer

Coburg resident Joe Laidman, who turns 92 in July, has lived in Queen St for just over 90 years. And he reckons that must be a record that few residents could match.

Mr Laidman has seen the street and surrounding areas develop from cow paddocks to thriving residential areas.

Mr Laidman ... was 18 months old when his parents moved to 1 Queen St where they operated a small grocery shop in the backyard. There were only three houses in the street.

'There was a house at number 1, 3 and 2,' Mr Laidman said. 'There were no more houses, just paddocks all around this area.'

'People would walk from Moreland Rd across a paddock to get to my parents' shop.' More houses were being built by the time Mr Laidman went to school.

He would earn pocket money by walking around the houses scattered around Sydney Rd taking orders from families. He would then help his mother pack the orders and deliver them.

'I'd have to walk about three-quarters of a mile to

• **Joe Laidman**

deliver the goods but when I finished I was allowed to play,' Mr Laidman said.

Come Saturday, with the sixpence he made during the week, he and a friend would walk to the Lyric Theatre ... to watch a film. Afterwards they would walk to Albion St to George Sand's Fish Shop to buy fish and chips.

'That was our entertainment for the week,' Mr Laidman said, 'and all on sixpence. The only way to get around was to walk.'

Mr Laidman remembers his mother walking him to Moreland State Primary School ... When he attended high school in The Avenue, he would walk down to the creek, cut across a vacant lot and through houses to get to

the school.

The first transport in the area that Mr Laidman can remember was a cab. 'You could walk faster than he could go,' he said.

When he began working in the city as a storeman, he would walk to Moreland Station or Sydney Road and catch the cable train, or ride a bike.

Having grown up in Queen St it seemed only natural that when he married in 1926 Mr Laidman would continue to live in the street.

'Never thought of living anywhere else,' he said.

Mr Laidman purchased a block of land at 51 Queen St.

'When I was single Dad told me to buy a block of land because by the time I

got married the land would be worth double,' he said.

'So I bought a double block in Saunders St and sold that and bought this (51 Queen St).

Mr Laidman recalls his future parents-in-law were not too impressed about where their daughter was to live.

'They said: "You can't go down and live there. That's in the bush. There's no houses around you" and they only lived in Albion St, East Brunswick.'

When he and his wife, Marjorie, build their house in 1926 there were houses on either side and a few house opposite.

While the house has had a few alterations and coats of paint over the past 68 years, Mr Laidman said that nothing could alter the memories.

'This house holds many, many memories for me,' he said, tears welling in his eyes, thinking of his wife, who died four years ago, and his son growing up.

'I hope I never have to shift out,' he said

(From The Courier, 9 May 1994. Reproduced with permission.)

Heritage haggling

Historic theatre to be demolished to make way for exciting new entertainment centre!

Greenhills council announced today that the historic Royal Theatre may be demolished to make way for a new entertainment complex next to the recently built sports and leisure centre.

Many residents are angry at the proposal. They say that the building is of important historical significance in the area. Many elderly residents have fond memories of visiting the theatre as children. The theatre is still used on Friday and Saturday nights but attendance is decreasing as more people watch movies on video or travel to the large cinema complexes in the city centre. The theatre was one of the first public theatres to be built in Greenhills and is still in excellent condition.

Other residents have argued that the entertainment centre will provide employment for many people and will offer young people a place to go after school and on the weekend. The centre will include video games and a fast food outlet. A public meeting has been called for next Friday night at the Greenhills town hall to help decide what to do.

All are welcome to attend.

HERITAGE HAGGLING ROLES

1. President of the Greenhills Historical Society

You are against the idea of the building being demolished. You are very interested in the history of Greenhills and you conduct tours of the old theatre for tourists. You do not think that Greenhills needs new places. You think it is important to hold on to the important places from the past.

2. Parent

You are against the idea of the theatre being demolished. As a child, you used to go to the movies every Saturday at the Royal theatre and you still take your grandchildren there. It is a part of your family life—a place to see friends and celebrate special occasions.

3. Teenager who lives in Greenhills

You love the idea of an entertainment centre being built in Greenhills. You often get bored on the weekends and you think this would be an exciting place to go. You think that Greenhills has too many old places and that there should be more modern, new places. You would like to get some part time work after school and you think there might be some jobs at the new centre.

4. Developer of the entertainment centre

Of course, you think that the entertainment centre would be a great idea. You know that it will make quite a bit of money and you have promised the historical society some of the money to help them maintain other old buildings. You have built an entertainment centres in other cities and they have been very popular

5. Councillor

You have not made up your mind about the problem. You are willing to listen to everyone at the meeting and to help people come up with some solutions. You think that the centre might be good for the young people in the area but you are a bit worried about demolishing such a precious old building.

UNIT 2

YOU, ME AND WE

A unit of work about cross-cultural understanding for lower primary

ABOUT THIS UNIT

The capacity to live with diversity is integral to modern-day living. Students need to develop, from very early on, skills and understandings which enable them to understand other cultures and to also become aware of themselves and their own culture in the process. This unit encourages young learners to consider diversity as central to their lives and to develop understandings about cultural diversity beyond the notions of 'us and them'. An important objective of cross-cultural awareness is to help students to live with difference and to continue to reconstruct their view of the world in the light of new information and experience. It is based on the premise that cross-cultural curriculum (in this case, a study of Asia) should be about 'reconstructing our self images and the images of others with a sense of proportion, an attention to diversity and in a critical frame of mind.' (Viviani 1991, p.8)

This unit aims to develop greater cross-cultural awareness through a comparative cultural study. Students are involved in comparing and contrasting another culture with their own, and in reflecting on the influences of other cultures on the society in which we live. The choice of South Korea for the comparative study is a deliberate means of highlighting the growing importance of the Asia-Pacific region in world affairs. The development of inclusive views of the world is enhanced through learning experiences which avoid exclusive emphasis on a Eurocentric perspective.

KEY TERMS

family	similar
work	different
celebrations	culture

UNDERSTANDINGS AROUND WHICH THIS UNIT IS BASED

Individuals belong to cultural groups.

The cultural group to which a person belongs influences their lifestyle.

Similarities exist between cultures in the nature and scope of family life, work, celebrations etc.

Differences exist between cultures in the nature and scope of family life, work, celebrations etc.

Living with difference is integral to life in modern day societies.

Many societies are made up from people from a range of different cultural groups.

KEY PERSPECTIVES IN SOCIAL EDUCATION

Thinking critically

The global society

Individual potential

Diversity and difference

Cultural heritage

Developing values

Spirituality

KEY LEARNING OUTCOMES FOR SOCIAL EDUCATION

Describes the ways in which people live their lives

Identifies similarities and differences in the lives of different cultural groups

Explores common and unique characteristics among individuals and groups

Gathers and records information from direct and indirect experiences of people and places

Describes practices, customs and traditions of familiar groups and communities and unfamiliar groups and communities

Identifies characteristics of their own culture

Reflects on the ways in which the characteristics of their own culture compare with the cultures of others

Prepares information for an audience

LANGUAGE OUTCOMES

Uses oral language to recount personal histories

Prepares simple oral and written texts for a familiar audience

Constructs meaning from visual texts

Uses language (oral, written and symbolic) to reflect on learning

SELECTION OF TEXTS

In this unit you will need to consider the range of texts (written, spoken and visual) needed for students to access information about their own culture and the culture of others. Some of these texts may include photographs, video material, discussions with guest speakers and questionnaires.

DEVELOPING A CRITICAL PERSPECTIVE

As students will be involved in the use of a wide range of texts, it is essential that they consider the messages these texts contain and the ways in which a number of meanings may be found in the same text if a critical perspective is applied.

Focus on genre: recount

This unit requires students to develop understandings about their own culture and the culture of others. It therefore lends itself well to the explicit teaching of recounts (factual, personal and imaginative). Students use recounts for accessing information and experience, and as models for the creation of written and oral recounts to process their understandings. The explicit teaching of this genre provides students with greater control over it and will add to their repertoire of oral and written language skills. This focus on genre is a 'unit within a unit' and we suggest you take time to focus on the modelling and application of the genre.

Note that the unit allows for the exploration of all three types of recount (personal, factual and imaginative). Their structure remains essentially the same, although they differ minimally in the type of language used.

KEY FEATURES OF THE RECOUNT GENRE

Purpose: A recount reconstructs an event or an experience.

Structure: A recount begins with an orientation, for example:

My name is Clare Cortez and I was born in Spain

and this is followed by a series of **events:**

When I was four my family came to live in Greenhills.

Language used: Usually the participants in a recount are specific as in this example with *Clare Cortez.* The simple tense is used, for example *I was born* and there is the use of action verbs such as *lived* and *moved.* There are linking words to do with time (*then, after that, next, before*). In personal recounts personal pronouns such as *I* and *we* are used; in factual recounts such as historical recounts the third person is used (*he, they,* and *she*); and an imaginative recount usually uses the first person.

TEACHING SEQUENCE: RECOUNTS

The following shows *one approach* to teaching key features of the information genre. For more detailed advice refer to Derewianka (1990) and Wing Jan (19910.

Teacher modelling: A range of models of recounts (written and oral) can be used as models. For this unit in particular, recounts which depict aspects of the local and/or other cultures, or a reconstruction of an event, for example a birthday party, or an imaginative recount of what life in another part of the world may be like can be used. These recounts allow students to access information, and also work as models for their own writing or oral recount. You may create a personal, factual or imaginative recount to use to model and demonstrate the key features of the genre to your students.

Spotlight on structure: The structure of a recount relates to the purpose of the text and its intended audience. Questioning students about the structure of the text allows them to focus on the particular structure of this genre and apply this to their own writing or oral language.

How is the written/oral recount structured?

Is there an orientation?

Is the orientation followed by a series of events?

Spotlight on language features: Language used in a recount helps to create the particular meaning of the text. A focus on how the language is used to create meaning enables students to choose language appropriate to this genre in their own written or oral language.

What pronouns have been used?

Are there any action verbs?

Have linking words to do with time been included?

Other things to consider:

Have you been able to locate accurate information?

Have you been able to include information relevant to your audience?

Will your audience understand your information?

Is your information accurate?

Have you included the most important facts and information?

PREPARATION

- Organise a learning log for each student (see chapter 3).
- Choose a place/culture for the comparative cultural study. This will, of course, depend on the resources available, but consideration should be given to a culture that contrasts significantly with many of the student's own.
- Collect a range of visual images which reflect cultural diversity at the global and local community level, for example images from magazines, photographs, newspapers (pictures of faces, people at work, houses and other buildings, environments, etc.). The use of visual images is integral to this unit, so a collection from a wide range of sources is advised.
- Organise a video/excursion/guest speakers that will inform students about the culture selected for comparative study.

TUNING IN: SAMPLE ACTIVITIES

PURPOSE

- to provide students with opportunities to become engaged with the topic
- to ascertain the students' initial curiosity about the topic
- to allow students to share their personal experience of the topic

1 Silhouettes

Trace around each student's head/profile. In each profile, students record their personal details as below. Begin the activity by modelling your own personal profile in a silhouette of your head, for example:

My name: Clare Cortez
Where I live: Australia
Where I was born: Spain
People in my family: Mum, Dad, Tom
Where Mother was born: Australia
Where Father was born: Spain
Things my family does together: birthday parties, holidays, shopping at the market
Language(s) spoken at home, school, with friends: English, Spanish
Important celebrations: birthdays, Christmas, New Year, name days

2 Photo gallery

Establish a photo gallery in the classroom. Students bring photos from home which reflect different aspects of their lives. Captions can be recorded under the photographs, for example:

Things I/we like, things I/we do
I am Clare and I like to ride my bike with my family
This is my family ...
We celebrate ...
On special occasions I ...

3 Same and different game (attribute matching)

Individually, students draw a range of activities in which they engage with family and friends, for example:

Draw some of the things you do at home/with your family

Draw some of the things you do at school

Draw some of the things you do in your neighborhood

These drawings are cut out and used for classifying activities. Students work in small groups and classify their drawings according to similar attributes, for example:

'Share your pictures with your friends. Now put your (combined) pictures into groups of things that belong together.'

Other images may be added to the collection to challenge and extend the attributes selected for grouping. Ensure that the collection of visual images of people is comprehensive and shows a balance of gender, age and ethnicity.

4 Game: Who is it?

Choose a student in the class and, without naming them, describe them so that other students can guess who you are talking about. Ensure that you describe them in positive terms and emphasise distinguishing traits and attributes. Avoid any tendency to describe them using physical features only. The student who guesses whom you are describing then selects someone to describe and so on.

5 Just like me

Provide students with photographs (from magazines, etc.) of people who may be different to them in some way—for example a young, female student from an Anglo-Saxon background could be given a photograph of an indigenous male adult to investigate. The aim of the exercise is for students to consider the similarities between themselves and the person in the photograph. Ask students:

How are you like the person in the photo?

Encourage a variety of responses, for example:

This man has a big smile like me.

Students work in pairs to discuss the similarities they have found and to suggest ideas to each other. Responses are shared with the whole class.

6 People bingo

Design a simple 'people bingo' sheet for students to complete (see chapter 3). This activity is designed to stimulate discussion about the various cultural experiences within the class. For example, categories could include:

Find somebody who celebrates their birthday with a party.

Find somebody who speaks more than one language.

Students move around the room questioning each other and filling in the spaces on the sheet with the name of the person who fits the category. Older students or independent learners may be able to complete the activity without guidance; however, some students may require support. Students could be paired up to move around the room together, finding people who match the category, or you could read each question or category out separately to younger students who could draw pictures of the person in the spaces provided.

7 Perfect match

Prepare a simple activity for students which involves them in matching a class member to a particular attribute, for example:

> *Someone who is always happy*
> *Someone who helps people*
> *Someone who cooperates*

PREPARING TO FIND OUT: SAMPLE ACTIVITIES

PURPOSE

- to find out what the students already know about the topic
- to provide the students with a focus for the forthcoming experience
- to help in the planning of further experiences and activities

8 Me and you

Show students a range of visual images which depict people of different, age, gender and ethnic background. Number each image. (Students record the numbers of the images they choose in their learning log so that this activity can be revisited at a later stage.) Ask students to record the images of people:

- they think are most like themselves and least like themselves
- they think live in their country
- they think they would like to get to know.

Some of these responses can be shared with the whole class.

9 Getting to know you

Questions are prepared for members of students' families, neighbors, friends of the family, etc. You could use the categories in activity 1 to help develop a list of suitable questions. Students may add questions of their own to the ones already prepared. The results of these questionnaires are collated for use at a later stage in the unit.

10 Oral histories (Focus on genre: recount)

Students give an oral presentation to the class detailing aspects of themselves and their family. The emphasis in this activity is to encourage students to talk about themselves in a meaningful way, using the guiding questions in activity 1. It will be necessary for students at this level to be taken through a number of demonstrations before they present their own oral history. Students may be used to presenting an aspect of themselves, for example during news time, but not be familiar with talking in greater detail about individual and **cultural** similarities and differences.

11 Structured learning log entry

Ask students to reflect on the input they have had so far about similarities and diversities that exist within their class and the wider community. Reference to the activities undertaken during the 'Tuning in' phase of the inquiry will provide a structure for this reflection. Students can draw/write/tell their responses, using the following questions as a guide:

What can we say about the people in our class? In what ways are they the same/different?

What can we say about the families of the people in our class? In what ways are they the same/different?

12 What do we know about South Korea?

Inform the students that they will be investigating life in South Korea (or a culture of your choice) and compare lifestyles (family life, work and celebrations) with their own. Find out what students already know about South Korea. They may tell you using written and oral language, picture or drama.

13 What do we want to know

Ask students to think about what they want to find out about South Korea—with particular emphasis on family life, work and celebrations. These questions can be recorded and asked of the guest speaker when they visit the class.

FINDING OUT: SAMPLE ACTIVITIES

PURPOSE

- to further stimulate the students' curiosity
- to provide new information which may answer some of the students' earlier questions
- to raise other questions for the students to explore in the future
- to challenge the students' knowledge, beliefs and values
- to help students to make sense of further activities and experiences which have been planned for them

14 Getting to know you: questionnaire

Design a questionnaire (or use the one developed in activity 9) for students to take home and bring the information they have collected back to class. It may be necessary to obtain the assistance of older brothers and sisters or friends in completing this exercise. In addition to this, students may wish to rehearse the questionnaire with a partner before taking it home.

15 Local walk

Walk around the local community to observe, discuss and record (taking photographs) evidence of cultural difference and similarity. Look for evidence of:

- the influence of other cultures on the community (restaurants, language, shops)
- individuality or diversity (for example, a house or a garden which looks distinctive)
- similarity in the community (for example, cars which look the same)
- community or places where people live, work or celebrate (for example, the local shops, parks, playgrounds, church)

16 Cultural study: South Korea

View and read:

Blackline master 8 depicts some key images of life in South Korea and provides some information about each one. Students compare and contrast these images with images of their own culture.

View:

View video material such as *Images of Korea* (Korea Foundation) as an introduction to family life, work and celebrations in Korea.

Look:

A range of photographic images about South Korea can help students to gather information about family life, work and celebrations.

Listen:

Students listen to a guest speaker provide them with a personal recount about South Korea. Aspects include: culture in South Korea, travelling in South Korea, living and working in South Korea, introduction to Korean language.

It may be possible to locate someone who is from South Korea, someone who has travelled to South Korea or someone connected to South Korea through an embassy or consulate to provide the students with additional information about the culture and family life, work and celebrations which shape the culture. Some useful addresses include:

- The National Korean Study Centre
  PO Box 218 Hawthorn
  Victoria
  Australia 3122
- Korea Economic Institute of America
  1030 15th Street NW
  Suite 62 Washington DC 20005 USA
- International Cultural Society of Korea
  Daewoo Building 5th Floor
  526, 5-ga Namdae-num dong
  Joong-ku
  Seoul Korea

17 Silhouette: 'This is Kim'

Read through ***blackline master 9*** on Kim from South Korea. (A possible sentences exercise could be used to introduce this blackline master—see chapter 3.) Students create profile of Kim from the information provided and make a silhouette similar to the ones they made for themselves. In creating the profile, the following questions can be used:

Where was Kim born?

Where does Kim live?

Who is in his family?

What things does Kim s family do together?

What language(s) is spoken in Kim s home?

What celebrations do Kim s family observe?

SORTING OUT: SAMPLE ACTIVITIES

PURPOSE

- to provide students with concrete means of sorting out and representing information and ideas arising from the 'finding out' stage
- to provide students with the opportunity to process the information they have gathered and present this in a number of ways
- to allow for a diverse range of outcomes

18 Who are we? Class profile

Students review the information about themselves recorded on their silhouettes in activity 1. This information is shared with the whole class and students create a class profile based on this information. This could be made into a book/wall display titled 'Did you know?' for example:

Did you know that all people in our class celebrate their birthdays?

Did you know that nine people in our class were born in another country?

Did you know that four people in our class speak another language?

19 Revisiting the photo gallery

Students review the images collected in activity 2 for the photo gallery depicting things they like to do alone, with friends and with family. Students can generate statements about themselves and themselves in relation to other class members with the following questions as a guide:

What can you say about yourself and the things that you do, the things that are important in your life?

What can you say about your family and the things that are important to them?

What can you say about other members of the class and what is important to them and their families?

20 Graphs and charts

Students review the information collected about their families, friends and neighbors from the questionnaire. A tally sheet such as the one below could be displayed on the classroom wall and used to collate the data for comparison and contrast.

Names

Places where they live

Number of people in the family

Places where mother was born

Places where father was born

Languages spoken at home

Work that people do

Things families do together

Once students have an understanding of the general nature of the information represented in the tally sheet, they can use mathematics to explore it in more depth. Simple bar and pie graphs can be created from the information tallied from the results of the questionnaire.

The following questions can guide the exploration:

How many people in our study were born in this country?

How many people were born in another place in the world?

How many people live in small families?
How many people live in large families?
How many people speak more than one language?
What is the most common work that people in our study do?
What is /are the most common things that families do together?
What is/ are the most common celebrations that people in our study have?

21 Using information from the local walk

Students use plasticine or other art materials to create visual representations of the things they noticed in their community that were the 'same' and 'different' during the walk in activity 15. A large mural could be displayed somewhere in the school or in the local community.

22 Revisiting images (1) South Korea

Revisit the images and information about South Korea (gained from **blackline master 8**, video or photographs.) Students compare and contrast these with the photo gallery created about themselves and their families.

What do these images tell us about life in South Korea?
What things may be important to children like Kim in South Korea?
What things may be important to families in South Korea?

Common and diverse elements in cultures can be studied using the understandings developed about life in South Korea in comparison with the profile of family and cultural life created in the classroom. Students may wish to draw themselves and their friends and families involved in family life, work or celebrations and cut these out. They can draw elements of Kim's life and sort these into the categories of 'same' and 'different'. Students can share their sorting and classifying with the whole class and discuss the results.

23 Dear Kim

Students write a letter to Kim telling about themselves and their families, responding to the information provided in **blackline master 9.** They can draw on the information provided in the silhouettes and the photo gallery to help them.

24 Culture capsule

This activity involves the students choosing things that represent aspects of their culture to show to people like Kim who live in other countries. Items could include images/photographs, descriptions/pictures of games or toys, wrappers from food containers, items of popular culture like basketball cards or music and so on. Ask:

What might you take in a suitcase to South Korea to teach Kim something about your culture?

25 Visual representation

Using the information in **blackline master 9**, together with the information they have gathered from videos or guest speakers, students create a visual representation of aspects of Kim's life (housing, play, family, celebrations, clothing, etc.).

26 Revisiting the images (2)

Revisit the images/photographs used at the beginning of the unit which depict people from a range of backgrounds, age groups and of different gender. Ask students to recall the responses they had to the questions relating to this activity. Discuss what understandings they have developed so far about people and the similarities and differences that might exist between them. These reflections can be recorded in the learning logs.

GOING FURTHER: SAMPLE ACTIVITIES

PURPOSE

- to extend and challenge students' understanding about the topic
- to provide for more information in order to broaden the range of understandings available to the students

27 Researching another culture

In pairs or trios, students now conduct a simple investigation of another culture. As a starting point, they could refer to the countries of birth indicated in the questionnaires and in the class profiles. The data chart below could be used to progressively record the information as it is gathered. It will be necessary for you to demonstrate the use of factual texts and the use of glossaries, contents pages and so on to help students conduct their research. Information could be categorised using the following headings as a guide:

> Name of country
> Where in the world
> Main language spoken
> Family life
> Work
> Celebrations
> Food
> Clothing

Students capable of independent work may search through books, magazines and newspapers to find out about people who live in other countries and the various aspects of their culture.

28 Think and observe

As a whole class, students consider the influences that people from other countries/cultures have had on their own lifestyle. As a simple starting point, observe items at home for their country of origin, for example 'Made in Korea', and make a list of these items. Lists of food, languages, music, celebrations such as Chinese New Year and so on from other cultures can be recorded and used as the basis for discussion. A mural could then be constructed depicting cultural elements that have been incorporated into local culture.

29 Same-town

In pairs, students consider the implications of living in 'Same-town' where no one is allowed to be different. These discussions could be shared in simple role-plays or in drawings, or stories where the characters and events do not

Figure 24 *'I liked the lion dance. I saw it on the video about Korea.'*

Figure 25 *'This Korean man has a special flute.'*

reveal any diversity. Following on from this, De Bono's PNI strategy (see chapter 3) can be applied where students consider what would be positive, negative and interesting about living in Same-town.

30 Walk in my shoes

If possible, locate some dialogue/conversation from an audio tape or video tape of the Korean language. Inform students that you want them to listen to a tape and tell you about what is on it. Do not tell them that the language is other than their own. Once they have listened to the tape they may consider the following:

> *What language was being spoken?*
> *What makes you think this?*
> *Did you understand anything?*
> *How did you feel when you were listening to it and you couldn't understand it?*

Ask students to consider what might happen to them if they went to South Korea to see Kim and they could not speak Korean? How might they feel? How might they cope with the situation? How might they communicate? Students may wish to recall events in their lives when they have come across people speaking other languages or times when someone is experiencing difficulty because they do not speak English.

MAKING CONNECTIONS: SAMPLE ACTIVITIES

PURPOSE

• for students to draw conclusions about what they have learnt
• to provide opportunities for reflection on both what has been learnt and on the learning process itself

31 Welcome Kim

Present a hypothetical situation to the students involving Kim coming from South Korea to stay with them. Ask students:

> *If Kim came from Korea to live with you, what would he see/feel/do/act?*
> *What might be the same for him, what might be different?*
> *What do you think he would like most about living with you, and what might he like least?*

Students could make a learning log entry where they draw/write about what Kim might experience if he lived with them.

32 Crossing the bridge

Role-plays are created around a hypothetical situation where students welcome Kim to their home, school or club. The scenario must take into account the fact that Kim speaks very little English and that the students speak no Korean, so that they need to consider how they will communicate cross-culturally without the aid of a common language.

33 Collage: the global village

Using images/photographs from newspapers, magazines and so on, students create a collage which depicts people with similarities and differences, common and unique elements of a culture, connections between people, influences from other cultures and so on. This collage could be made in the shape of the world and students could add statements of understandings about the unit of work to the collage.

TAKING ACTION: SAMPLE ACTIVITIES

PURPOSE
- to assist students to make links between their understandings and their experience in the real world
- to enable students to make choices and develop the belief that they can be effective participants in society
- to provide further insight into students' understandings for future unit planning

34 Share with others

Invite parents and grandparents to participate in a sharing of the understandings developed throughout the unit. This could involve a hypothetical 'birthday party' for all students in the class. Food, decorations, clothing, and music associated with a birthday celebration across cultures forms the basis of the party.

35 Global village display

Display the global village created by the students in activity 33 in a location where others in the school community can be informed about the content of the unit.

36 Putting you in the picture

Using the strategy outlined in chapter 3, students reflect on learning about themselves and others.

INFORMATION ABOUT SOUTH KOREA

This is the flag of South Korea. The circle in the middle represents the people. The white background represents the land. The black bars represent heaven, earth, fire and water.

The language spoken in South Korea is Han-gul.

호랑이도 제 말하면 온다

Some people in the countryside might live in a courtyard house. There is more room in the countryside for these kinds of houses.

Many people in South Korea live in apartments in big cities. The capital city in South Korea is Seoul.

Many people in South Korea have to eat kimchi. Kimchi is made from different types of vegetables. It can be bought in a store or made at home.

Many different sports are played in South Korea. Tae-kwon-do is a favorite sport. It was developed in South Korea over 2000 years ago.

Sometimes people in South Korea wear traditional clothes. They might wear these clothes for special occasions such as weddings.

Many things are made in South Korea and exported to countries all around the world.

Nike

SAMSUNG

Hyundai

GOLDSTAR

I am Kim

Hello, I am Kim. I was born in South Korea and I am eight years old. I live in Seoul which is the capital city of South Korea. Many, many people live in this city. It is very crowded, with lots of cars, trucks and buses. My family lives in a small apartment. We have three rooms for my mother, my father, my sister and me.

I go to school on the bus every day. At school we like to play soccer or basketball. I am learning English—the alphabet and some words, and when I grow up I hope to study English at high school. I can also play the drums.

Sometimes we visit my grandmother and grandfather in the country. We take the fast, modern train and it takes about three hours to get there. My grandmother and grandfather live in a small house with a tiled roof. They have chickens in the backyard. My grandmother makes us kimchi which is our favorite food. Kimchi is made from lots of different vegetables and Korean people like to eat this every day. Grandma puts the kimchi in pots all around the house—even on the roof! She also dries garlic, peppers and ginger and she hangs these on string in front of her house. We go to the market with her to buy fresh fish for dinner.

On weekends, my family goes for picnics in the mountains. We take our lunch with us—rice, kimchi and fish. My sister and I like to run fast up the mountains, but my mother and father like to walk behind us. We take our kites and fly them. Sometimes we go for a holiday in the mountains and we take our tent. The mountains are peaceful and my father says he likes to go there so he can get out of the city.

My father works in a department store in Seoul and my mother used to teach music. Now she is at home with my little sister. My mother tells me lots of stories about when she was a little girl living in the country. She says that South Korea has changed a lot since then.

Sunday is a special day for visiting our family and friends. When we have special occasions like a wedding, my mother wears her Hanbok. This is a traditional dress and it is made of beautiful colored material. My father wears traditional clothes too. He wears a jacket (Jeogori) over pants (Bagi) . We have two very special celebrations in South Korea. One is the celebration for New Year and the other is called chusok which is held in August. Chusok is a celebration of the rice harvest and it goes for three days. We eat special rice cakes at this time.

UNIT 3

BEHIND THE SCENE

A unit about popular culture for middle and upper primary

ABOUT THIS UNIT

This unit explores the nature and scope of popular culture. It involves students in examining aspects of popular culture that influence their lives and the lives of other generations. Students come to an appreciation of popular culture through engaging in activities which identify and value the culture of their time. Popular culture is examined as both a symbol of change and a recurring theme amongst generations.

Students are also encouraged to examine the influence of popular culture on their lives and asked to think critically about the ways in which they are targeted to think, dress and act in accordance with a particular code. Critical readings' of popular culture involve students in uncovering the meanings embedded within media (television, radio, film, magazines) and seeing how these messages are fashioned for particular audiences. Emphasis is also given to the tensions created between individual choice and collective consciousness.

While this unit views popular culture as something integral to the lives of different generations, it also acknowledges the power involved in creating and recreating what is acceptable and what is not. It is hoped that the unit may help some learners to identify and explore their own feelings of self-worth and belonging in acknowledging the pressure of the mainstream. It is essential that students are aware of the transient and cyclical nature of popular culture and the struggles that may involve them in 'daring to be different' at this time in their lives.

KEY TERMS

popular culture	marketing	messages
advertising	individual	influence
peer group	symbols	media

UNDERSTANDINGS AROUND WHICH THIS UNIT IS BASED

Elements of culture that are deemed fashionable and contemporary are often defined as 'popular' culture.

Popular culture influences many aspects of people's lives.

There are many vehicles for advertising and sustaining popular culture—including television, music and clothing. This advertising is often directed at young people.

Although popular culture is constantly changing, many elements of popular culture are repeated in later generations.

Generally, popular culture affects the lifestyles of young people.

People both shape and are shaped by popular culture.

Symbols of popular culture are used to achieve status or power and to persuade others.

People who choose to resist or challenge popular culture are sometimes treated negatively.

KEY PERSPECTIVES IN SOCIAL EDUCATION

Making choices and taking action

Imagining and constructing the future

Thinking critically

Individual potential

Time, place and space

Developing values

KEY LEARNING OUTCOMES IN SOCIAL EDUCATION

Interprets accounts and artefacts of different people at different times

Constructs a sequence of some major periods and events

Identifies and reflects on key influences on choices they and others make in their everyday lives

Compares and contrasts characteristics of the popular culture of one generation to the next

Links some historical events with the emergence of popular culture

Critically analyses the intent behind advertising

Uses a range of media to communicate ideas to and influence others

LANGUAGE OUTCOMES

Uses written and oral language to persuade

Analyses everyday texts (television, radio, magazines, newspapers)

Provides examples of the way that the language of popular culture can include and exclude

SELECTION OF TEXTS

You will need to consider the range of texts (written, spoken and visual) needed to help students to access information about popular culture. Texts could include magazines, newspapers, photographs, television programs, video material, music, advertisements and so on.

DEVELOPING A CRITICAL PERSPECTIVE

As students will be involved in using of a wide range of texts, it is essential that they consider the ways in which these texts are constructed to give the audience a particular message. Attention to the meanings created by these texts involves the students in developing a critical perspective.

Focus on genre: persuasive written and oral language

This unit requires students to focus on the meanings generated by various aspects of popular culture and the ways in which an audience is targeted. It therefore lends itself well to the explicit teaching of persuasive oral and written language; thereby allowing students to use their understanding about persuasive language to access information and use as a model for the creation of persuasive texts to process understandings. Explicit teaching provides students with greater control over this genre and will add to their repertoire of oral and written language skills. This focus on genre is a 'unit within a unit' and we suggest you take time to focus on the modelling and application of the genre.

Note that it is of particular relevance to the genre of persuasion that attention is given to the ways in which visual texts (photographs, images, advertisements and so on) provide the viewer with powerful messages.

KEY FEATURES OF PERSUASIVE WRITTEN AND ORAL LANGUAGE

Purpose: Persuasive written or oral language (and visual texts) attempt to convince others about a particular point of view. Beliefs are made clear (or they can be quite subtle) and may be biased or skewed to a particular viewpoint only.

Structure: Persuasive written or oral language begins with a **statement of a particular viewpoint or position**, for example:

Children exercise common sense in their viewing of video material.

This is followed by an **argument** or series of arguments which support this position:

It is common for young children to walk away from video material that upsets them.

Finally the position is **summed up** and this may involve restating a number of points or could use an analogy or metaphor or the like:

Videos are not the problem, the level of violence in society is of more concern.

Language used: Usually the reference in a persuasive text is generalised, for example *Videos are not harmful to children.* Different types of verbs are used — action verbs (*watch* and *switch*) some linking verbs (*are* and *is),* some saying verbs (*state* and *explain*), and mental verbs (*believe* and *hope*). Some technical terms may be used, for example *virtual reality.* Persuasive texts are mainly constructed in timeless present tense: *Videos make a lot of children happy,* and frequently the passive tense: *A survey may be used to prove this.* Language associated with reasoning is used, for example: *What harm could they possibly do?* And this language is connected to the argument with words like *so, therefore, as a result.* Frequent use of emotive words such as *should* and *unreasonable concern* are included.

TEACHING SEQUENCE: PERSUASIVE WRITING

The following shows *one approach* to teaching key features of the genre of persuasion. For more detailed advice refer to Derewianka (1990) and Wing Jan (1991).

Teacher modelling: A range of models of persuasive writing and oral language can be used. For this unit, newspaper articles, advertisements (print and media), jingles, excerpts from political speeches, slogans and so on may be used. These persuasive texts allow students to focus on the meanings generated in a persuasive text and also work as models for the students' own writing or oral language. You could create your own persuasive text to model and demonstrate the key features of the genre to your students.

Spotlight on structure: The structure of a persuasive text (written or oral) relates to the purpose of the text and its intended audience. Questioning students about the structure of the text allows them to focus on the particular structure of this genre and apply this to their own written or oral language.

> *How is the written/ oral text structured?*
>
> *Does the persuasive text begin with the statement of a belief or position?*
>
> *Does an argument or series of arguments follow?*
>
> *Is there a summing up of the belief or position?*

Spotlight on language features: Language used in a persuasive text helps to create the particular meaning of the text. A focus on how the language is used to create meaning enables students to choose language appropriate to this genre in their own written or oral language.

> *How is the language persuasive/ What words and phrases are used? Are they emotive? Do they appeal to reason?*
>
> *Have you used words to connect arguments?*
>
> *What tense is used?*
>
> *What is included and what is left out?*

Other things to consider:

> *Will the audience be persuaded by your writing/talk?*
>
> *Have you used words/phrases and sentences to persuade the audience?*
>
> *Is what you are saying possible/realistic?*

PREPARATION

- Organise learning logs for each student.
- Collect items of popular culture.
- Consider guest speakers for the 'finding out' stage.
- Record advertisements and television shows for relevant activities.
- Contact gallery/museum about possible excursions.
- Design draft research contract.

TUNING IN: SAMPLE ACTIVITIES

PURPOSE

- to provide students with opportunities to become engaged with the topic
- to ascertain the students' initial curiosity about the topic
- to allow students to share their personal experience of the topic

1 Getting started

Students respond to the following questions, using words and/or pictures. Keep their responses for reference later in the unit.

> *Who would you most like to be like?*
>
> *If it was your birthday tomorrow, what gifts would you like to receive?*
>
> *What would you like to do really well? (e.g. sport, music)*
>
> *If you could, what would you change about your appearance? Why?*

2 Jingle quiz

Prepare a tape of short excerpts from current advertising jingles from radio and television. Organise students into small groups and explain that you are going to play them a series of jingles and they must decide, as a group, what the jingles are advertising. They write down their responses after each one.

1. I would love to be Janet Jackson...
2. I would really wonna meet culture for my Birthday Party
3. I would really love to be a sexy model
4. My body I want a perfect body to be a nice model and for cute guys..

This activity could become a mock quiz with you as the host of the show. After the quiz, groups share and check their responses.

Discuss some of the issues and ideas arising from the activity:

How did you know the products these jingles were advertising?

What did you notice about the jingles?

Do you think your parents/ grandparents would have been able to do this activity? Why?

Who found the task difficult? Why?

Who found it easy? Why?

3 Culture on display

Bring some artefacts that represent aspects of current popular culture. Examples might include:

basketball cards

popular item of clothing

toy/game/gadget

teenagers' magazine

picture of current teenage celebrity (sports star, musician, TV personality)

container or wrapper from popular junk foods etc.

Display the items somewhere in the room and pose the questions:

What do all these things have in common?

What do they tell us about things that are currently popular?

Could you add to the display?

The display should be developed throughout the unit.

4 Graffiti board

Begin a graffiti board in the classroom on which students make a list of current popular sayings or words—within the bounds of decency of course!

5 Who's cool?

Ask students to draw pictures of a typically 'cool' person (i.e. someone who is currently fashionable/popular). Ask students the following questions as the basis for a general discussion. Tape the discussion for later use.

How do you know that these things are cool?

Who decides what is cool?

What choices do we make about things that are fashionable or popular?

Figure 27 *Children list popular sayings and words on a graffiti board*

6 Bedroom survey

Students investigate their bedroom. Ask:

Are there some things that you once really wanted and now you do not use or even like?

Students could bring along sample items to share with the class and explain their reasons for no longer liking or using the item. Discuss what this says about popular culture.

7 Out in the cold

Ask students to reflect on a time when they felt they didn't belong to a group—or when they felt left out or unpopular. Reflective entries may be written in learning logs with the option given to share the entry or excerpts from it.

In reading over their recollection of this time, ask students to consider why they might have felt left out. Was it because they were different from others in some way? How did it feel? How did they deal with this time? (Examples could include being ostracised because of the clothes they were wearing, the food they had for lunch, the fact that they didn't have a particular toy, etc.)

PREPARING TO FIND OUT: SAMPLE ACTIVITIES

PURPOSE

* to find out what the students already know about the topic
* to provide the students with a focus for the forthcoming experience
* to help in the planning of further experiences and activities

8 Time capsules

In small groups, students nominate the contents of a time capsule that is designed to represent aspects of the current popular culture. Explain that the time capsule could be found by their children or their grandchildren. The jingles that you played to them in the 'tuning in' activity 2 could be one of the items.

Each group must come up with:

1. One song or piece of music
2. One item of clothing
3. One item of food
4. One example of a leisure-time activity
5. Two contemporary heros (one male, one female)
6. One television program
7. One book or magazine
8. One hairstyle
9. A list of popular words and phrases

Figure 28 *Students could design and make a popular 'dictionary' for their time capsule*

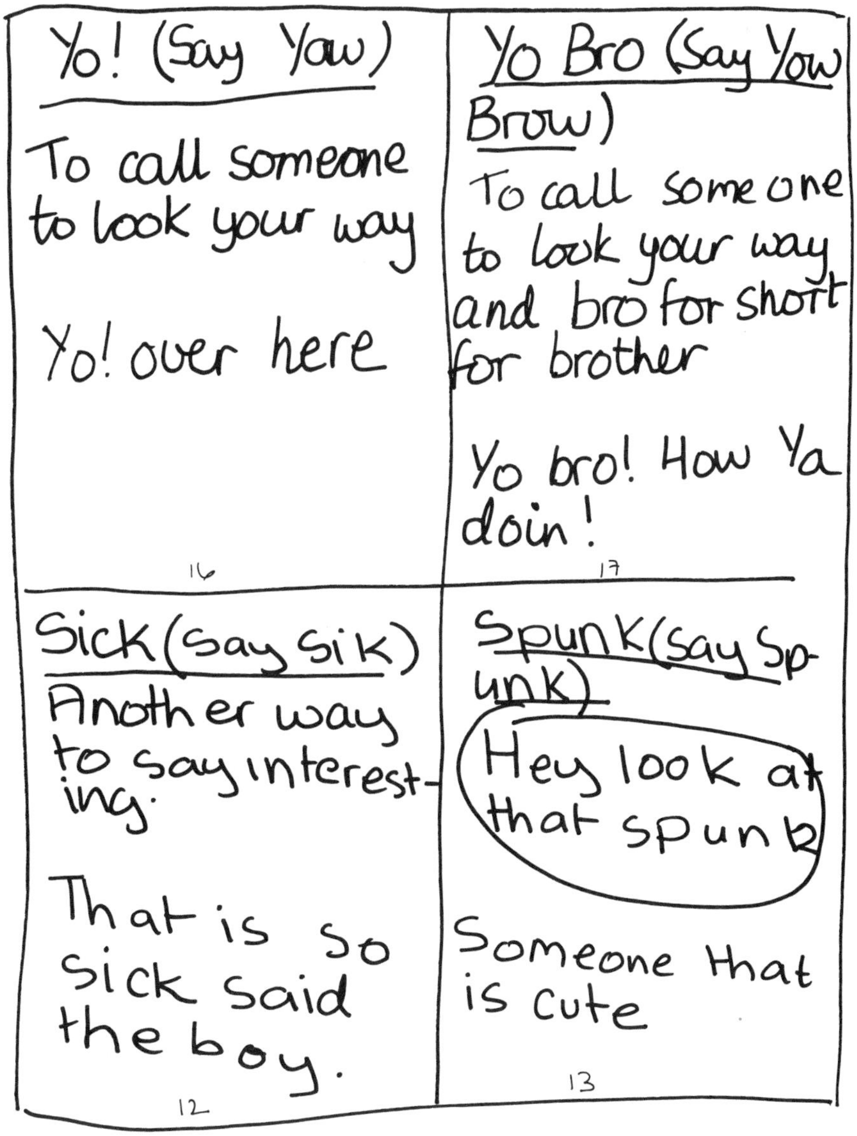

Yo! (Say Yow)	Yo Bro (Say Yow Brow)
To call someone to look your way	To call some one to look your way and bro for short for brother
Yo! over here	Yo bro! How Ya doin!
16	17
Sick (Say Sik)	Spunk (Say Spunk)
Another way to say interesting.	Hey look at that spunk
That is so sick said the boy.	Someone that is cute
12	13

The groups will have one week to compile their capsule, using photographs, tapes etc.

At the end of the week, a session should be set aside for each group to share their time capsule. They need to explain why they nominated each item as representative of the popular culture of their time. Having shared the ideas for a time capsule discuss:

What are the common links between the items that we have selected?

What are the key reasons behind our selections?

What would people think about us if the time capsule was opened? Why?

Ask students to consider the kinds of items that they might find if they were to open a similar time capsule that had been put together when their parents were young people. In the same groups, students make a list of possible items and again share them and discuss. Ask students:

What items do you think we would find?

Why are the items different from those you have selected for your own capsule?

Why do you think this?

What evidence remains of this popular culture?

9 What do we know about advertising and popular culture

Share with students an advertisement for a highly popular item—it can be a magazine, television or radio advertisement. Provide the following focus questions and ask students to reflect on them in their learning logs. The purpose of this activity is to find out what students understand about the nature of advertising. The teacher should accept all responses at this stage.

Why do you think this advertisement was made?

Who do you think was involved in making it?

Figure 29 *Students respond to focus questions on advertising in their learning logs*

ADVERTISING

What do we know?

1. Advertisements make you buy things
2. Big letters advertise better than small letters
3. You have to use exiting words in advertisements
4. Advertising presents businesses
5. Sometimes advertising is on T.V., in newspapers and on some more things
6. Advertising is on posters and signs
7. Advertising can be commercial
8. Advertising tries to persuade you
9. Advertisements are nearly everywhere
10. Advertisements are a lot of fun!

What is it selling?

Who is it aimed at?

How does it try to convince you?

How does it make you feel?

What kind of language is used to capture your attention or influence you?

What is the meaning conveyed in the advertisement, and how is the meaning created?

Share responses by swapping learning logs. Encourage students to read at least two other logs. This activity will provide you with some information on students' understanding of the nature of advertising and the use of popular symbols to persuade others.

10 Questions for a guest speaker

Prepare a list of questions for and predictions about a guest speaker who will come to talk to the class about advertising. Ask: *What would we like to find out from our guest speaker? What do we think he/she might say?* This could be done using a 1-3-6 strategy (see chapter 3).

11 Preparing surveys

Explain to students that they will be gathering information about the way popular culture has changed over time. In small groups and then as a class, design a survey to give to older people. Samples could be taken from those who were young people in the 40s, 50s, 60s, 70s and 80s. Sample questions are included on *blackline master 10*. These questions could be modified and also asked of older teenage students.

FINDING OUT: SAMPLE ACTIVITIES

PURPOSE

- to further stimulate the students' curiosity
- to provide new information which may answer some of the students' earlier questions
- to raise other questions for the students to explore in the future
- to challenge the students' knowledge, beliefs and values
- to help students to make sense of further activities and experiences which have been planned for them

12 Talking to the people

Conduct the interviews prepared in activity 11. This task could extend for some weeks over the unit. Students could interview one person from each age group, or each age group could be allocated to different teams of students. You may need to spend some time with students practising interview skills. Encourage students to seek permission to record their interviews.

13 Guest speaker

Invite a guest speaker in to talk to the students about advertising. Examples of the sorts of people who might be appropriate include someone who:

is involved in the advertising industry in general

negotiates to sell advertising space in the media

teaches in the area of media studies (e.g. a lecturer at a local college)

is involved in promoting/selling a popular product

works for a popular magazine

14 Playground observation

This activity requires students to observe their peers at play and to note the influences of popular culture that may be at work on their interactions. The task could involve simple, unstructured observations made during outdoor play or could be a more formal task involving checklists or even video cameras.

Begin by taking the class out together to watch younger children at play. Encourage the students to note the types of activities they are involved in and any influences they think might be at work on this play. The following format may be useful for recording observations:

Observation	Possible influences
Using American accents	American television shows
Rap dancing	Video clips
Kicking, play fighting, etc.	Video games, televised sport
Clothing/hairstyle	Television shows, heroes/heroines

Observing their peers or other students in this way may also precipitate discussion about the influences on students' own play. Discuss the kinds of activities that students engage in during their leisure time. Are they able to isolate the things that might be influencing their own play?

15 Case study: television

The programs

Select a popular television program that portrays young people. Most appropriate for this activity would be evening soaps pitched at young people. This activity is designed to begin to help students read the culture being portrayed by the program, and would best be done as a whole class using a video-tape or excerpts from the program. Set up a data chart using the following headings. The program could be stopped regularly for discussion and additions to the data chart.

What do the young people wear in the program?

What do they look like (hairstyles, etc.)?

What do they eat?

What kinds of music do they listen to—or is played as theme or background music?

What are some common phrases or words used by the young people in this program?

How do the young people relate to each other and to adults?

Now ask students to nominate a similar program to study in their own time. Results are brought back to the class and added to the data chart.

The advertisements

Ask students to keep a record of the advertisements shown during the programs they watch. This could be done using the programs selected for the activity above or may be a larger project carried out over a week. Students could focus on the following:

- link between type of program and product being advertised
- number of advertisements per program
- nature of products advertised
- target audience
- words/slogans used
- male/female characters
- age group of characters

These items could be entered onto individual tally sheets or onto a whole class chart

16 Excursion

Museums and art galleries often have exhibits that trace changes in popular culture over time. This could form the basis of a class excursion.

SORTING OUT: SAMPLE ACTIVITIES

PURPOSE

- to provide students with concrete means of sorting out and representing information and ideas arising from the 'finding out' stage
- to provide students with the opportunity to process the information they have gathered and present this in a number of ways
- to allow for a diverse range of outcomes

17 Pictorial timeline

Using the data gathered from the interviews and other experiences, students develop a timeline of popular culture around the room. Beginning with the 1940s, for example, ask students to represent their information in visual form. They can use photographs, artwork, quotes from their interviews, etc. Invite parents and friends in to add ideas to the timelines. This visual representation can be added to throughout the unit. As the timeline builds, ask students: *What patterns do you notice?* (For example, the fashions of the 70s may be seen repeated in some of the fashions of the 90s).

Once the timeline has been established, ask students to consider the following question: *What can we say about what was happening during these times?* (For example: 1940s—Second World War, big bands, jazz, etc; 1960s—Vietnam war, Woodstock, peace movement, etc.)

Encourage students to use reference materials to add some of the key historical events to the timeline.

Can links be made between some of these important events and people and some of the fads and fashions that emerged?

18 Revisiting the advertisements

Following the guest speaker's visit, return to the advertisement used in activity 9. Frame the questions again to students and build on or modify ideas. Students now make some generalisations in response to the question: *What can we say about advertising and how and why it influences us?*

19 Reading advertisements

Select another advertisement for a popular product (e.g. soft drink, sport). Demonstrate how to 'read' this advertisement (see questions in activity 9) with the whole class. Students then use advertisements they have collected and work in small groups to 'read' them in the same way. Introduce the term 'marketing', as this is modelled.

20 Reading images

An extension of this activity may be to examine the ways in which advertisers aim to influence boys and girls. Ask students:

> *What is a 'boy's' advertisement? What is a 'girl's' advertisement?*
> *What image of boys and girls do the advertisements portray?*
> *How do these images relate to your own images of yourselves?*

21 Role-play

Students return to the notes made during observations of children at play in activity 14. Using the data gathered from playground observations, ask students to prepare small scenarios of children at play. In preparing their scenarios, they must select an aspect of popular culture that may have influenced that play. Other students then analyse their performances accordingly. Alternatively, cards depicting common items of popular culture (e.g. particular TV personalities, sporting heroes, items of clothing, games, music) could be placed in a lucky dip. Students then select cards and these must be used to inform their 'play'.

Figure 30 *Children role-play aspects of popular culture that influence their play*

22 Get with it

Having viewed and analysed aspects of popular teenage television programs (see activity 15) ask students to analyse their own lives using the same set of questions. Now ask:

How similar/different are we to the kids who are portrayed on the television?
Why?
What kinds of influences do those programs have on us?
What evidence is there of this influence?

Explore the notion of the 'unpopular' within the context of these programs. What isn't shown or said? Who isn't represented? Devise a mural showing the 'ins' and 'outs' according to a certain program. On the 'in' side are all the acceptable items, sayings, actions, appearances, etc. On the 'out' side are things that would be considered unacceptable by the mainstream peer group on the program. Ask:

What language do we use to describe people who are 'out' of the popular group?
What reasons may there be for people being 'outside' the popular group?
Do we have a choice?

23 Visual representation

Using the data gathered about advertisements run during popular TV programs (see activity 15), students represent the information using graphs or other appropriate diagrams. Ask: *What do these graphs tell us?*

GOING FURTHER: SAMPLE ACTIVITIES

PURPOSE

- to extend and challenge students' understanding about the topic
- to provide for more information in order to broaden the range of understandings available to the students

24 Research groups

Students are organised into small research groups. Each group is assigned a particular aspect of popular culture and must examine that aspect from both a historical and a contemporary perspective. An important aspect of this research should be the **images** and **messages** associated with the popular culture of the time. Groups design a research contract to carry out over a given period of time.

Research topics:

popular music
popular clothing and hairstyles
popular radio
popular film
popular reading material (comics, magazines)

Each group conducts their investigation around the following focus question:

How and why has this aspect of popular culture changed over the last 50 years?

Data may be gathered through interviews, library searches (books, photographs), and memorabilia.

MAKING CONNECTIONS: SAMPLE ACTIVITIES

PURPOSE

- to assist students to draw conclusions about what they have learnt
- to provide opportunities for students to reflect both on what they have learned and on the learning process

25 Culture creation

Examine the ways in which a particular aspect of popular culture (e.g. a television program, a currently popular movie, a toy or item of clothing) has been marketed by advertising companies. Ask students:

What is this marketing attempting to do?

What is the role of advertising in this process?

Who benefits from this marketing?

As a class, decide on a simple item, word or activity that is not currently popular but is easily accessible. How could you, as a class, introduce the word or activity into the popular culture of the school? Talk about some possibilities such as:

a new collectable item

introducing a new word to mean 'great' or 'terrific' (this could even be made up)

a new item of clothing or a new way of wearing something

Observe over time the way other students react. Discuss:

Does the initiative catch on?

Is it rejected? Why? Why not?

How do new entries into our popular culture take a foothold?

What helps/hinders their acceptance?

Why do they change?

26 Who's cool now?

Refer to the discussions of who's cool held in activity 5. Now ask:

Who decides what is cool?

What choices do we make about things that are fashionable or popular?

27 Using popular culture

In small groups, give students the task of making something unpleasant or unpopular seem exciting or attractive using some of the symbols of popular culture they have been exploring. They will need to consider the best way to market their 'product' and persuade their audience. Some possible forms of expression include:

a piece of art in the popular style of the time

a rap song

an excerpt from a popular television program

a fashionable piece of clothing with a relevant slogan

Possible focus for performance:

road safety	doing the dishes
toothpaste	school
homework	

Invite parents and friends to view the performance pieces. Each group must explain the nature of their piece and give a 'behind the scenes' interview with the audience at the end.

28 Imagining the future

Ask students to think about the possible characteristics of popular culture that might exist when they are adults.

What changes do they think might occur in society?

What might popular culture 'look like' in the future? Why?

What current trends might return?

Ideas can be presented orally, visually in written form or through drama.

29 What have we learnt?

Ask students to reflect in their learning logs on the question:

What does it mean to say that someone is a 'slave' to popular culture?

TAKING ACTION: SAMPLE ACTIVITIES

PURPOSE

- to assist students to make links between their understandings and their experience in the real world
- to enable students to make choices and develop the belief that they can be effective participants in society
- to provide further insight into students' understandings for future unit planning

30 Dare to be different

Have a 'dare to be different' day. Each child is conscious of their behaviour within the peer group and actively tries to resist influences. Reflect on this at the end of the day.

31 Making choices

In the light of this unit, ask students to review some of the responses they made to the focus questions provided early in the unit. Are they now able to understand more clearly the influences on their choices? Would they change any of their responses now? Why?

32 Public debates

Hold a public debate in the school about related topics, for example:

Television advertising has a bad influence on young people

Everyone should wear school uniforms

Pop music today is better than the popular music of our parents' generation

Students use written and oral language to attempt to persuade their audience.

POPULAR CULTURE SURVEY

What was your favorite song when you were young / a teenager?

What was your favorite band / group?

What was a popular dance?

What kinds of clothes were fashionable?

What hairstyles were fashionable?

Was there a popular car? What was it?

What was a book / magazine that young people read?

What was your favorite film / television program?

What did you like to do with your friends?

Did you have a favorite hobby or pastime? What was it?

UNIT 4

FAMILIES IN FOCUS

A unit about the changing nature of family life— adaptable to all levels

ABOUT THIS UNIT

Exploring the topic of families is instantly relevant to most students. Whilst perceptions of family life vary enormously, this is a unit to which all students can bring ideas, and some prior experiences. Teachers, therefore, have the most significant resource for teaching right there in the classroom — in the lives and experiences of the students they teach.

'Families in focus' provides a powerful opportunity to develop understandings about the shared and diverse elements within our society. This unit challenges students' perceptions of what a 'family' is and leads them to realise that their own experience may be very different from that of others. At the same time, activities ask students to look for patterns and similarities across this diversity. It picks up on common themes of conflict and cooperation, roles and responsibilities, and develops students' skills and strategies to cope with day-to-day problems and issues that arise.

Finally, the unit fosters reflective and thoughtful responses to the topic, encouraging students to think of their role within a family and of the things that others in the family do to support them.

KEY TERMS

change	diversity
conflict	independence
cooperation	beliefs

UNDERSTANDINGS AROUND WHICH THE UNIT IS BASED

There are many different types of families in our society.

Families differ in many ways, and these differences may be linked to culture, race, beliefs, environment and socioeconomic status.

While there are many differences between families, they also share some common characteristics, needs and structures.

People in families often have particular roles, jobs and responsibilities.

Family life changes from generation to generation.

Conflict is often a part of family life. Families have different levels and sources of conflict and deal with it in different ways.

Rituals and celebrations are a common aspect of family life all over the world.

KEY PERSPECTIVES IN SOCIAL EDUCATION

Making choices and taking action

The global society

Individual potential

Thinking critically

Justice, rights and responsibilities

Cultural heritage

Changing lifestyles

Spirituality

Developing values

KEY LEARNING OUTCOMES FOR SOCIAL EDUCATION

Identifies similarities and differences in the lives of different generations

Describes different periods of time

Critically interprets accounts and artefacts from other times

Sequences a set of events in chronological order

Identifies, reflects on and analyses aspects of family life that have endured or changed

Portrays an event or occasions from different perspectives

Describes different views held by individuals and groups about issues related to family life

LANGUAGE OUTCOMES

Uses written and oral language for the purpose of reflecting on ideas, feelings and beliefs

Justifies ideas, feelings and beliefs

Interprets meanings from text and illustrations contained in simple narratives

Communicates ideas and understandings through drama and role-play

SELECTION OF TEXTS

You will need to consider the range of texts (written, spoken and visual) needed to help students to access information about different types of families. Some of these texts could include stories, photographs, discussions with guest speakers, newspapers and magazines.

DEVELOPING A CRITICAL PERSPECTIVE

As students will be using a wide range of texts, it is essential that they consider the importance of analysing this information and experience with a critical perspective, particularly as the status of family life is constantly undergoing change and redefinition.

Focus on genre: reflection

This unit requires students to develop understandings about different families. It therefore lends itself well to the explicit teaching of the reflection genre; thereby allowing students to use reflections for accessing information and experience, and as models for the creation of written and oral reflections to process understandings. Such explicit teaching provides students with greater control over this genre and will add to their repertoire of oral and written language skills. This focus on genre is a 'unit within a unit' and we suggest you take time from the unit of work to focus on the modelling and application of the genre.

KEY FEATURES OF THE REFLECTION GENRE

Purpose: A reflection enables the writer or the speaker to make sense of an experience.

Structure: A reflection begins with an experience, for example:

> *My family always loved to go on holidays down at the beach.*

and includes **opinion** about the experience:

> *I believe these were the best times we had.*

Language used: The participants in a reflection can be generalised:

> *Families are interesting.*

or specific:

My brother David was always shy.

Mental verbs (*think, feel, believe,*) are used in relation to the opinion and judgement and pronouns can be first person (*I* and *my*) and third person (*we, they, he* and *she*).

TEACHING SEQUENCE: REFLECTION

The following shows *one approach* to teaching key features of the information genre. For more detailed advice refer to Derewianka (1990) and Wing Jan (1991).

Teacher modelling: A range of models of reflection (written and oral) can be used. For this unit in particular, reflections such as diary entries, conversations, interviews with guest speakers, autobiographies and biographies, and stories may be used. These reflections allow students to access information, and also work as models for their own written or oral reflections. You could create your own reflection to use to model and demonstrate the key features of the genre to your students.

Spotlight on structure: The structure of a reflection relates to the purpose of the text and its intended audience. Questioning students about the structure of the text allows them to focus on the particular structure of this genre and apply this to their own written or oral language.

How is the written/oral reflection structured?

Is there an orientation?

Has opinion been included?

Spotlight on language features: Language used in a reflection helps to create the particular meaning of the text. A focus on how the language is used to create meaning enables students to choose language appropriate to this genre in their own written or oral language.

What pronouns have been used?

Are there any mental verbs?

Other things to consider:

Do you wish to show your reflection to an audience other than yourself?

Has your reflection enabled you to outline your beliefs and feelings?

Has your reflection enabled you to make sense of your beliefs and feelings?

PREPARATION

- Gather photographs or memorabilia of your own family (immediate, past and extended).
- Write to the parents of students in the class to inform them of the unit topic and the activities in which students will be engaged. Set a date for the 'family day' at the end of the unit.
- Investigate any video material that may be available from your local resource centre (see suggestions in unit).
- Gather picture story books that deal with diverse family types, conflict and roles.
- Organise guest speakers.

Figure 31 Students begin the unit by sharing family photographs and starting a class gallery

TUNING IN: SAMPLE ACTIVITIES

PURPOSE

- to provide students with opportunities to become engaged with the topic
- to ascertain the students' initial curiosity about the topic
- to allow students to share their personal experience of the topic

1 Family snaps

Begin the unit by sharing photographs of your own family with the students. You should select photos to cover a wide definition of the term—beyond the immediate family. Include, if possible, cousins, grandparents, pets—even very close friends you regard as being 'like family'. It is important at this stage to avoid implying narrow definitions of what a family is so as to allow students to feel comfortable about the particular structure or composition of the group they call their 'family'.

Now ask students to bring in some photos of people in their family and begin a class gallery. Students add a caption to any photos they display. The emphasis here is on providing opportunities for students to feel comfortable about sharing ideas and experiences of family life. Stress that there are some things people are happy to share but others we prefer to keep to ourselves. It is important to set up an atmosphere of trust amongst the classroom community early in the unit.

2 Bulletin board

Gather articles from the newspaper/magazines, etc. which explore issues concerned with the family. Continue this throughout the unit.

3 A classroom visitor

Invite an elderly friend to talk to students about memories of his/her family life. A similar activity is suggested in the 'finding out' stage but it may also be useful to spark interest here. Alternatively, you could dress up as an elderly person or take on a character from a book. Wander into the classroom after lunch and begin to tell students about your memories of your family. You live alone now ... Encourage the students to ask you questions.

4 Images of the family

Collect and display images of family life (photos, paintings, etc.) around the room. Encourage students to talk about what they see in the images. What kinds of messages about families do they portray? How does this message compare to their own feelings about families? How do the images differ? Why?

PREPARING TO FIND OUT: SAMPLE ACTIVITIES

PURPOSE

- to find out what the students already know about the topic
- to provide the students with a focus for the forthcoming experience
- to help in the planning of further experiences and activities

5 What is a family?

Use a 1-3-6 consensus strategy (see chapter 3) to explore students' perceptions of what a family is. Retain individual and group records for assessment purposes. This activity may be extended by asking students to gather definitions from other people (parents, friends, etc.). Display these ideas around the room. Look for patterns and discuss differences.

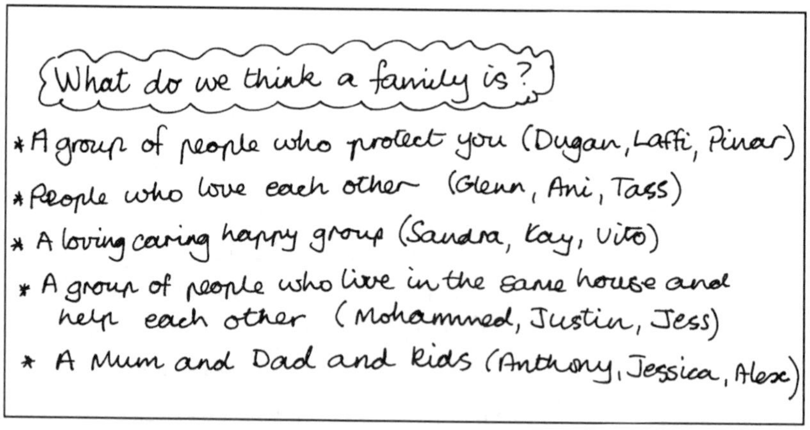

Figure 32 *Students will have different ideas about what a family is*

{ What do we think a family is? }

* A group of people who protect you (Dugan, Laffi, Pinar)
* People who love each other (Glenn, Ani, Tass)
* A loving caring happy group (Sandra, Kay, Vito)
* A group of people who live in the same house and help each other (Mohammed, Justin, Jess)
* A Mum and Dad and kids (Anthony, Jessica, Alex)

6 Mapping our ideas

Concept mapping: Students construct a draft concept map to highlight their current ideas about families (see chapter 3).

7 People bingo

Use the people bingo strategy (see chapter 3) to help students find out a little more about each other's families. Ensure that the instructions on the sheet are inclusive and reflect the diversity within your class. Some ideas might include:

Find somebody who lives with one other person

Find somebody whose family speaks two languages

Find somebody who has lived in more than two homes

Find somebody who has more than 5 people in their home

Find somebody who has a family pet

8 Making models

Provide students with modelling clay or plasticine and ask them to make a model of:

(a) a family

(b) their own family

As students are working, move around the room asking questions and sharing ideas with individuals:

Tell me about your model. What are you trying to show?

Is this your family? Tell me who this is. What did you want to show about them?

Where are you in the family? How are you going to model yourself?

9 Structured brainstorm

In groups, students brainstorm responses to key questions:

Why do we have families?

What do families need?

What do families do?

How are families different? [Some families ... but others ...]

How are families the same? [Most families ...]

10 Scenes from family life

Students mime various scenes of family life (fictitious or based on their own). Examples include:

breakfast time

watching TV

getting ready to go on a trip

visiting relatives

doing chores

11 Preparing a survey

Design a survey (see chapter 3) to gather more detailed information about the families in the class, school or community. Agree on a list of questions relating to family members, jobs, activities, conflict, changes in the future. Be sure to remind students that information will be shared with others and should only include elements that interviewees are comfortable to share.

12 Listing questions

Generate a list of questions about families. This could be done through a structured brainstorm (see chapter 3) using the following headings:

Questions about roles in families

Questions about parents and children

Questions about different types of families

13 Direct analogies

Brainstorm some 'direct analogies' (see chapter 3), for example: 'How is a family like our school?', 'How is a family like a circus?' Create new metaphors for the family throughout the unit.

FINDING OUT: SAMPLE ACTIVITIES

PURPOSE

- to further stimulate the students' curiosity
- to provide new information which may answer some of the students' earlier questions
- to raise other questions for the students to explore in the future
- to challenge the students' knowledge, beliefs and values
- to help students to make sense of further activities and experiences which have been planned for them

14 Surveys

Using the questionnaire designed in activity 11, students gather data about their own and/or other people's families.

15 Video

There are numerous videos that either indirectly or directly explore the theme of family life. You should view all videos first to ensure suitability and relevance to the students. Examples include:

Songs of Innocence: A child's view of family life, Australian Children's Television Foundation, 1993.

Relevant excerpts from the well known *7-up* series (Michael Apted, BBC).

16 Guest speaker

Invite a guest speaker or panel of guests (parents, grandparents, other teachers, older children, etc.) to share information about their families and family life. Prepare questions prior to the visits.

17 Local walk

Conduct local walks to find out where various members of the class live. If possible, some homes could be visited.

18 Families through literature

Select relevant literature to read with students throughout the unit. There are countless children's books which explore themes related to family life. Select those focusing on diversity, conflict resolution, change and family roles. Some worthwhile examples include:

Armitage, R. & Armitage, D. *When Dad Did the Washing*, Andre Deutsche.

Base, G. *My Grandmother Lives in Gooligulch*, Nelson.

Brady, T. *Nobody's Granny*, Ashton Scholastic.

Brown, A. *The Piggy Book*, Julia Macrae Books.

Browne, A. & McFee, A. *The Visitors Who Came To Stay*, Hamish Hamilton.

Burningham, J. *Avocado Baby*, Jonathan Cape.

Fox, M. *Wilfred Gordon McDonald, Partridge*, Omnibus.

Gretz, S. *It's Your Turn Roger*, Dutton.

Hunt, N. & Niland, D. *Families are Funny*, Collins.

Levinson, R. *I Go with My Family to Grandma's*, Orchard Books.

Loh, M. *Tucking Mummy In*, Ashton Scholastic.

Say, A. *Grandfather's Journey*, Houghton Mifflin.

Wild, M. & Hannay, L. *Sam's Sunday Dad*, Hodder & Stoughton.

As books are read, a comparative chart could be set up to record the various images of family life they portray. This table can be added to using information gathered from survey data

Title of book	No/names of people in the family	Good times	Family problems	Ways of solving problems

SORTING OUT: SAMPLE ACTIVITIES

PURPOSE

- to provide students with concrete means of sorting out and representing information and ideas arising from the 'finding out' stage
- to provide students with the opportunity to process the information they have gathered and present this in a number of ways
- to allow for a diverse range of outcomes

19 Representing survey data

A simple way to help students sort survey data is to cut each survey sheet up into numbered responses. Place responses to same questions in piles (e.g. all responses to number 1 go together, all responses to number 2 go together and so on). Now assign a small group to each question from the survey. They must read through each response and decide on the best way to represent the results to the rest of the class (see *blackline master 11*). Some examples include:

How many people are there in your family?	Tally these results and present them on a graph.
What jobs do people in your family have?	Tally the results and present information on a graph or chart. It could also be shown through representative pictures in magazines.
What are some of the things your family likes to do together?	Make a mural showing from most to least common, the sorts of things families do together.

What are some of the things that cause conflict?

Tally results and then choose the most common issues to role-play to others.

Imagine your family in ten years' time. Do you think it will be different? How?

Tally responses and write a report about changing families for the class.

Figure 33 *Students sort their data by cutting up the survey sheets and grouping responses*

20 Drama/art or language — responding to interview

A number of processes could be used to sort out information gathered from guest speakers. Discuss highlights of the visit and the similarities and differences between the guests' ideas about family life. Add to the retrieval chart (above) using information gathered from guests' stories. Retell and illustrate their stories. Write a biography of one of the speakers and publish it (with their permission) in the school newsletter.

21 Role-play: solving problems

Develop scenarios based around common sources of conflict that have been generated in the 'finding out' stage. Students act out these scenarios and show different ways they could be resolved. Sample scenarios are included in *blackline master 12*.

GOING FURTHER: SAMPLE ACTIVITIES

PURPOSE

- to extend and challenge students' understanding about the topic
- to provide for more information in order to broaden the range of understandings available to the students

22 Families far away	Using books, videos, picture sets or guest speakers, find out about family life in another culture. It may be appropriate to focus on a culture to which many students belong in the school. Draw out the similarities across cultures (celebrations, roles, structures of families) and the differences between these.
23 Families in change	Older students may gather some statistics about changes in family patterns over time from the Bureau of Statistics. Record these on charts and graphs. Discuss the reasons why these changes have occurred.
24 Families in song	Set up a listening post of songs that have been written portraying aspects of family life which relate to the unit's understandings. These should be selected carefully—simply being 'about families' is not enough. The content should be in line with the understandings and with students' needs.

MAKING CONNECTIONS: SAMPLE ACTIVITIES

PURPOSE

- to help students draw conclusions about what they have learnt
- to provide opportunities for students to reflect both on what they have learnt about the topic and on the process of learning

25 Making generalisations	Individuals and then small groups devise statements of generalisation about families and family life. These statements are then tested against each other, ordered or challenged. They can also be used for cloze activities with a focus on the content words. Again, return to concept maps, charts, definitions, statements, drawings and models, and ask students to examine their work and to make comments on how their ideas have changed and why.
26 Laying it on the line	By this stage in the unit, students should be aware of the range of values underlying people's opinions about and perception of families. This activity asks students to consider their own values. Read out 'startling statements' about families to students—they must decide on the extent to which they agree with that statement and stand on a line accordingly (see chapter 3). For example: 'Small families are better than large families', 'A family doesn't need to have children'. Individual students are 'interviewed' along the line to justify their particular viewpoint.
27 Family futures	On a timeline, students plot some significant moments in their family's past, then they predict some of the significant moments that may occur in the future. Compare these and look for patterns. Ask: *Why do you think this will happen?* Students could write a reflection to accompany the timeline.

28 Big book

A big book can be compiled to represent the similarities and differences between the families of students in the class. This could be done using the statements of generalisation generated by the students themselves. For example, 'Most families celebrate things together' could be supported by a range of examples from the grade: 'Sam's family celebrates birthdays', 'Voula's family celebrates Greek Easter' etc.

TAKING ACTION: SAMPLE ACTIVITIES

PURPOSE

- to assist students to make links between their understandings and their experience in the real world
- to enable students to make choices and develop the belief that they can be effective participants in society
- to provide further insight into students' understandings for future unit planning

29 Bringing it all back home (language focus: reflection)

Ask students to reflect on the role they play in their family. How do they feel about that? What can they do to enrich their role in family life?

The end of the unit is a time for reflection and action. The kind of action that students choose to take will depend very much on their particular family situation. The above questions could be the basis for some reflective writing, a letter to parents, other siblings, or simply a class discussion. It is important to help students see that the learning they have done over the course of the unit can be used in a positive way in their home lives.

30 Time to say thank you

Ask students to reflect on people in their immediate and wider family and to list all the different ways in which they care for them. Choose one person to write a letter of thanks to.

31 Self-reflection

Students complete the self-assessment and reflection using the questions below or a version of the self-assessment sheet given on *blackline master 13*.

> *What is the most important thing I have learnt about families?*
> *What is one thing I have learnt about myself in my family?*
> *What would I still like to find out about families?*
> *What activity helped me the most? Why?*
> *What piece of work am I most satisfied with? Why?*
> *How would I rate myself as a group member?*

32 Family day

Host a 'family day' where students invite people from their family to see all the work they have done about the topic. Set the room up as a gallery and devise a catalogue of exhibits. Students take their family around the room explaining their work.

SURVEY DATA

1. How many people are there in your family?

Task:

- Read through all the answers to this question. As you read, you should sort the answers out and make piles of answers that belong together.
- Your job is to make a graph to show others the different sizes of families that there are in this class.
- When you have finished your graph, answer the following questions:

  What is the most common family size in our class?

  What is the smallest family size?

  What is the largest family size?

- Write the answers in full sentences and display them near your graph.µ
- Now think about this:

  What are all the good things about having a small family?

  What are all the good things about having a large family?

- Brainstorm your ideas on the chart.

2. What jobs do people in your family have?

Task:

- Read through the answers to the question.
- As you are reading, sort the answers out into piles.
- What patterns do you notice for fathers? What patterns do you notice for mothers? What about brothers and sisters?
- Use the magazines to make a collage for each person. You must try to find pictures that show some of the jobs that have been written in the answers.
- Label your collage.

3. What are some of the things your family likes to do together?

Task:

- Read through all the answers to the question.
- As you are reading, put the answers in piles of those that belong together in some way.
- Your job is to make a mural that shows families doing all the different things that are in these answers. You need to talk about the mural first and decide who will do what.

4. What are some of the things that cause conflict in families?

Task:

- Read through the answers that you have been given. As you read, you could put the answers in piles of those which belong together for some reason. What things do families argue about the most?
- Your job is to make up one or two short plays to show some of these situations where families are in conflict. Imagine that you are about to be filmed for television — so your acting needs to be good!
- Practise your play carefully.

5. Imagine your family in ten years' time. Do you think it will be different? How?

Task:

- Read through the answers. How are they the same? How are they different?
- Your job is to write a story about how one family changes over the years. It might be your family or it might be one that you make up. When you have finished your draft, come to us for checking before it is typed onto the computer.

SOLVING PROBLEMS IN THE FAMILY

Characters: Child, mother, father
You try to convince your parents that you want more pocket money each week. They want you to do more around the house but you feel you do enough already.

Characters: Two friends
Your friend's parents won't let her go on school camp because they are worried about her safety. She has asked you what she should do.

Characters: Father, sister, mother, brother
Everyone in the family wants to watch something different on TV. There is only one TV in the house. How will you solve the problem.

Characters: Grandfather and grandchild
You are worried about your grandfather living by himself. You try to convince him to come and live with the family but your grandfather wants to stay at home.

Characters: Older sister, younger sister
Your older sister is planning to run away. She tells you but she doesn't want your parents to know. What will you say?

Characters: Father, brother, younger sister
Your dad wants you to take your little sister to the movies with your friends but you don't want her to come. How will you solve the problem?

Characters: Parents, sister, brother
Your parents think you should do more housework. You both want to send more time with your friends. How will you solve the problem?

THINKING ABOUT MY LEARNING

How well did I work as a member of a group?

_____

Reasons:

1 _____

2 _____

How well did I work on my own?

_____

Reasons:

1 _____

2 _____

How well did I join in whole class discussion?

_____

Reasons:

1 _____

2 _____

How well did I manage my time?

_____

Reasons:

1 _____

2 _____

Overall, I'd give myself the following rating for today's work.

_____

0   1   2   3   4   5   6   7   8   9   10

UNIT 5

A unit of work about decision-making and leadership for middle and

ABOUT THIS UNIT

Decision-making is essential not only for the effective and efficient operation of communities but also for the quality of people's lives as individual members of any group. Each day, people are faced with numerous situations, dilemmas and problems. It is the way they think, choose and act upon these moments that helps determine the kinds of lives they lead and the way in which others perceive and interact with them.

This unit explores the ways in which decisions are made, both at a personal and informal level and at the more structured and formal level through systems of government. It is a worthwhile vehicle for identifying and formulating codes of behavior for and management of the classroom community.

The unit encourages students to examine decision-making as a concept, as well as the skills involved in decision-making. Students also investigate the lives of people who have significantly impacted on the decisions others have made, comparing their own experiences of leadership with those of recognised world leaders. The unit moves back and forth between the personal, local and global context—examining patterns and connections throughout. Links are drawn between the structures for decision-making at home and at school and within local and national government systems. Importantly, students are challenged to think critically about leaders, leadership and decision-making.

KEY TERMS

decision-making
leadership
government
choice

UNDERSTANDINGS AROUND WHICH THE UNIT IS BASED

Decision-making is central to all aspects of people's lives.
People can affect and be affected by the decisions of others.
Decision-making is a complex process. People can develop skills and understandings to make more informed decisions.
Within any society there is a range of thoughts, beliefs, attitudes and opinions which, in turn, affect the way people act.
An individual's identity is often linked to the ways in which they participate in society.
Democratic systems are based on the ideal that all people can participate in decision-making. The success of this decision-making depends on people's commitment to the rights and responsibilities of all and the access they have to the decision-making process.
There are a number of factors that can help or hinder the effective participation of groups and individuals within a community.
Governments in democracies are established to assist in the management of society.

KEY PERSPECTIVES IN SOCIAL EDUCATION:

Making choices and taking action
Imagining and constructing the future
Thinking critically
Individual potential
Justice, rights and responsibilities
Developing values
The global society

KEY LEARNING OUTCOMES FOR SOCIAL EDUCATION

Describes the roles, rights and responsibilities of groups and individuals
Illustrates links between rights and responsibilities
Describes how rules are made
Interprets values inherent in people's motives and actions
Describes the basic features of political structures at local and global levels
Identifies the roles and responsibilities associated with leadership
Analyses the cause and effect of personal, community and global decisions
Applies understandings about decision-making processes to our personal life
Understands the rights and responsibilities of active participation in a local and global community
Reflects on the consequences of personal decision-making
Critically analyses different styles of leadership

LANGUAGE OUTCOMES

Uses written and oral language for the purpose of reflecting on ideas feelings and beliefs
Prepares oral and written reports for an audience
Justifies ideas, feelings and beliefs

SELECTION OF TEXTS

You will need to consider the range of texts (written, spoken and visual) needed to help students to access information about decision-making and decision-makers. These could include autobiographies and biographies, speeches, discussions with guest speakers, newspapers and magazines, television and video material.

DEVELOPING A CRITICAL PERSPECTIVE

As this unit of work involves students in the use of a wide range of texts such as those listed above, it is essential that they consider the importance of analysing this information and experience with a critical perspective; particularly as decision-making relies heavily on the ability to weigh up information and to make choices based on this information.

Focus on genre: reflection

This unit requires students to develop understandings about decision-making and decision-makers. It therefore lends itself well to the explicit teaching of the reflection genre, allowing students to use reflections for accessing information and experience and as models for the creation of written and oral reflections to process their understandings. The explicit teaching of reflection provides students with greater control over this genre and will add to their repertoire of oral and written language skills. This focus on genre is a 'unit within a unit' and we suggest you take time from the unit of work to focus on the modelling and application of the genre.

KEY FEATURES OF THE REFLECTION GENRE

Purpose: A reflection enables the writer or speaker to make sense of an experience.

Structure: A reflection begins with an experience, for example:

After deciding to buy a dog

and includes an **opinion** about the experience:

I realised the responsibility involved in caring for a pet.

Language used: The participants in a reflection can be generalised:

Some people do not take adequate care of their pets.

or specific:

I had thought about getting a pet for months.

Mental verbs such as *think, feel, believe,* are used in relation to the opinion and judgement, and pronouns can be first person (*I* and *my*), and third person (*we, they, he* and *she*).

TEACHING SEQUENCE: REFLECTIONS

The following shows *one approach* to teaching key features of the information genre. For more detailed advice refer to Derewianka (1990) and Wing Jan (1991).

Teacher modelling: A range of models of reflection (written and oral) can be used. For this unit in particular, reflections such as diary entries, editorial comment, autobiographies and biographies, or an interview with a politician may be used. These reflections allow students to access information and experience and also work as models for their own written or oral reflections. You could create a reflection to use to model and demonstrate the key features of the genre to your students.

Spotlight on structure: The structure of a reflection relates to the purpose of the text and its intended audience. Questioning students about the structure of the text allows them to focus on the particular structure of this genre and apply this to their own written or oral language.

How is the written/oral reflection structured

Is there an orientation?

is there reference to the event or experience?

Has opinion been included?

Spotlight on language features: Language used in a reflection helps to create the particular meaning of the text. A focus on how the language is used to create meaning enables students to choose the language appropriate to this genre in their own written or oral language.

How are the participants referred to?

What pronouns have been used?

Are there any mental verbs?

Other things to consider:

Do you wish to show your reflection to an audience other than yourself?

Has your reflection enabled you to outline your beliefs and feelings?

Has your reflection enabled you to make sense of your beliefs and feelings?

PREPARATION

- Organise a learning log for each student. Some activities are specifically designed to be documented in the log, but students should be encouraged to reflect in their logs regularly.
- Ask students to begin collecting newspaper articles that deal with issues about which a decision needs to be made. These may focus on individuals making decisions, local issues, national or global events. Also collect articles about formal government decision-making.
- Consider guest speakers for the 'finding out' stage
- Consider a possible excursion to local or state government offices.
- Record excerpts from televised parliamentary proceedings.

TUNING IN: SAMPLE ACTIVITIES

PURPOSE

- to provide students with opportunities to become engaged with the topic
- to ascertain the students' initial curiosity about the topic
- to allow students to share their personal experience of the topic

1 Teacher modelling

Begin by modelling a decision-making process aloud to the students. For example:

I'm trying to decide where to go on my holiday but I can't seem to make up my mind! Could you help me? What do you do when you have a decision to make?

2 Decision timeline

Ask students to reflect on the day so far. *What are some of the decisions you have made?* Share some as a whole class, then ask individuals to show some of the decisions on a timeline. This could be done using 'think' or 'speech' balloons in comic strip form. Share timelines and discuss the kinds of decisions we have to make during the day. How are our decision timelines the same and different?

3 Theatre sports game

Students work in pairs. Ask them to develop an impromptu role-play—a dialogue about making decisions. Give them simple scenarios such as those listed below. Every few minutes, intervene with a new variable that changes

Figure 34 *Decision timelines*

the nature of the dialogue and the decision-making process (these can be placed in a hat and drawn out periodically). Once students have experimented with a few dialogues, they 'perform' some of their role-plays to others.
For example, two friends discussing:

What game are we going to play at recess time?

What is the best television show?

What is the most fashionable piece of clothing you can buy at the moment?

What film will we go and see?

What will we make for dinner?

Who should we vote for at the next election?

Variables could include:

Now show the same decision being made between two people who have just met, or between two people who dislike each other

Discussion between a child and adult

One person wants the decision made in a hurry, the other can't make up their mind

An aggressive and a passive person.

These variables can be thrown in at any time during the role-play.
Discuss:

How did you go about the decision-making process?

What made it difficult?

What made it easy?

How and why did the different variables affect the process?

4 An important decision: (focus on genre: reflection)

Ask students to select an important decision they have made in their life. They write a reflection on this in their learning logs using the model outlined at the beginning of the unit. The following questions could act as a guide:

What was the decision about?

Why was it important?

What were all the things you had to think about when you were making the decision?

What did you choose to do?

What were the consequences of your action?

What do you think about that now? Would you change your decision if you could? Why?

Note that you could begin this activity by modelling a reflective piece about an important decision you have made in your life (e.g. deciding to be a teacher, deciding where to live). Refer to the section 'Focus on genre: reflection' to help you to discover the key features of reflections. Emphasise that the piece will be shared with others so that students select something they are happy to be made public.

Figure 35 Students reflect on decisions they have made

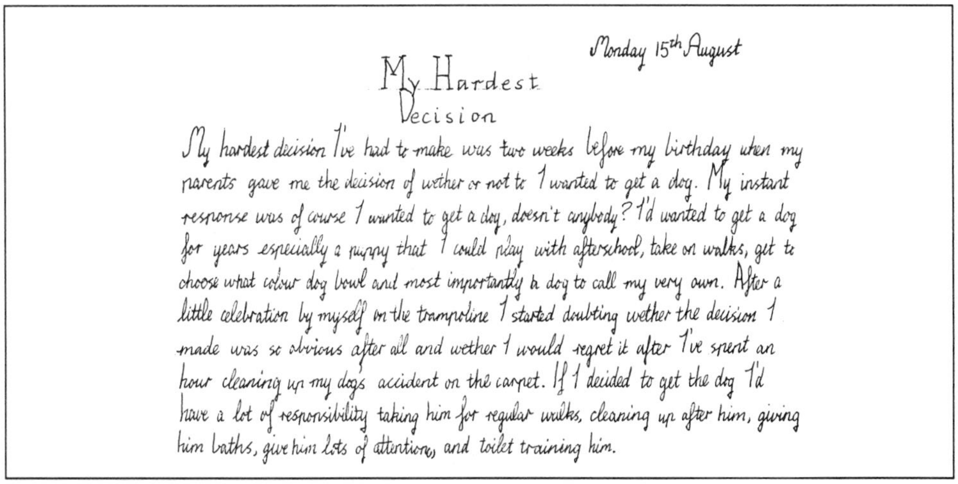

Monday 15th August

My Hardest Decision

My hardest decision I've had to make was two weeks before my birthday when my parents gave me the decision of wether or not to I wanted to get a dog. My instant response was of course I wanted to get a dog, doesn't anybody? I'd wanted to get a dog for years especially a puppy that I could play with afterschool, take on walks, get to choose what colour dog bowl and most importantly a dog to call my very own. After a little celebration by myself on the trampoline I started doubting wether the decision I made was so obvious after all and wether I would regret it after I've spent an hour cleaning up my dogs accident on the carpet. If I decided to get the dog I'd have a lot of responsibility taking him for regular walks, cleaning up after him, giving him baths, give him lots of attention, and toilet training him.

5 Laying it on the line

Give students simple, startling statements such as those listed below. They must decide where they stand in relation to that statement (e.g. on a scale of one to ten, from 'strongly agree' to 'strongly disagree'). This can be represented by asking students to stand along a long piece of string that is held across the room (see chapter 3). Any statements can be used for the activity; the emphasis is on the way we make decisions and the influence of others on our decision-making. Some sample statements:

All animals should be protected

Homework should be banned

Children should be able to do what they want

Private schools are better than state schools

'Interview' some students along the line about their reasons for choosing their particular decision. Discuss the things that influence the decision-making process during the game. This may also be done as a written activity.

6 People priorities

Provide students with a list of people that they must rank in order of importance. Ask them to include themselves on the list. Do not give any additional criteria at this stage. Once initial ranking has been done, students compare and discuss their ranking with others. With the whole class, discuss the following:

Whom did you put first? Why? Why is your first choice different from that of others?

What can we say about the ways in which we make decisions? What may we be basing our decisions on?

Now repeat the activity, this time ranking the people according to the positive contribution they have made to the world. Students share their list with others. With the whole class, discuss the following:

Whom have we placed as the people making the most positive contributions to the world?

How do we explain the similarities and differences in our choices?

On what criteria may we be basing our decisions ?

Select people with whom students are familiar to make the list.

7 Literature search

Select literature which illustrates the main character/characters involved in having to make a decision of some kind. For example, a central character may have to make a decision about whether to keep a secret from a friend, or may have to face certain consequences when others find out the secret they have long held. Some suitable books which focus on secrets and the decisions involved in keeping them form others include *Tuck Everlasting* by Nancy Babbitt, *The Last Week in December* by Ursula Dubosarsky, and *Finders Keepers* by Emily Rodda. Excerpts from these books which highlight the use of reflective language will be useful. Look at the ways in which the writer has tried to make sense of the experience and weighed up the options.

PREPARING TO FIND OUT: SAMPLE ACTIVITIES

PURPOSE

- to find out what the students already know about the topic
- to provide the students with a focus for the forthcoming experience
- to help in the planning of further experiences and activities

8 Brainstorming: graffiti sheets

Set up scribble sheets around the room with the following headings:

Leadership

Politics

Making decisions

Rights and responsibilities

Citizenship

Conflict

Power

Democracy

Students move around the room writing ideas that come to mind in response to that word. Small groups then take one sheet and analyse the overall response. Encourage them to look for patterns: *What have people said? What stands out? What questions arise?* Each group prepares a short report for the rest of the class.

Groups could also devise a concept map based on the ideas arising from the scribble sheet. These are then shared with the class. If students are completely unfamiliar with the words, simple definitions could be provided before beginning the activity.

9 Concept mapping

Using the list of key words above, groups or individuals attempt to map the connections between them. This map should be reviewed regularly during the unit.

10 Decision maps

Ask students: *When have you had to make important decisions for other people? When have you been in a position of leadership?* (e.g. at school, with younger siblings,

Figure 36 *Students write ideas that come to mind in response to particular headings*

outside school activities, clubs, etc.) Students construct a decision map to explain their situation and the way their decision affected those other people. Share these as a class and isolate some of the key things that help and hinder decisions.

11 Celebrity heads game: influential people

A student is given the name of an 'influential person' (e.g. well-known political figures, world leaders, school principal) who is familiar to them. This person's name is written on the blackboard above their head—in view of others in the class, but not the student.

Names used should include a wide range of people in leadership positions or positions of influence (not just political). Be mindful of a balance in gender, ethnicity and age.

Students ask the rest of the class questions that elicit a yes/no response to try to guess who they are. At the end of the game ask: *What do all these people have in common?*

12 Looking at leaders

Ask students: *Who are some of the leaders that you know?* (in our school, in our community, in the world). List these individually, then in groups. Conduct a magazine/newspaper search to find pictures of leaders and paste in a collage. *What makes a good leader?* Students compose a visual image of an 'ideal' leader, using a range of art materials including old magazines. They should identify the area in which that person is a leader and comment not only on the physical attributes but on the personality traits they think they should have. Now compare and contrast pictures and ideas. Ask students:

> *What features do our leaders have in common?*
> *What is the gender balance amongst our leaders?*
> *What ethnic backgrounds have we portrayed?*
> *What age are our leaders?*
> *What is the most common personality trait we have identified?*
> *What issues have we suggested our ideal leaders would be concerned about?*
> *Do you know of any 'real life' leaders that fit this image? Do you know other leaders who are quite different?*

In summary, discuss: What can we say about our beliefs and attitudes towards leaders? Why do we think this way? Where may our beliefs and attitudes come from?

13 Profiles of world leaders

Signal to students that they will be researching a world leader later in the unit. Negotiate possible people for their research. Together, develop a list of questions to guide the research:

> *Who are they?*
> *When and where were they born?*
> *How did they rise to a position of leadership?*
> *What were/are some of their beliefs?*
> *What is/was one of the important decisions they have made?*

How have they acted on this decision?
What were the consequences of this decision for them and for others?

14 Data chart

Ask students:
What are the current issues that need decisions in our school? In our community?
In the state? In our country? In the world?
Use the headings below to brainstorm an issue as a whole class and compile a data chart. Students then select another issue to be decided upon, of importance to them, and analyse in the same way. Reflect on the value of this exercise in helping clarify and resolve issues. (Headings: place, issue, people involved, possible solutions, possible consequences).

15 Preparing for an interview

Prepare a list of questions to ask a guest speaker—or a panel of speakers—who is in a position of leadership (e.g. from school, local community, local government). Involve students in organising these visits through letter writing, phone calls, etc.

16 What do we know about our government?

To prepare students to find out more about their system of government, ascertain their prior knowledge using the following strategy:
Set up four boxes in the room, each labelled with a different question:
Why do we have a government?
What do governments do?
Who are some of the politicians you know? What are their responsibilities?
How do governments make decisions?
Individually, students write their responses to each question on a piece of paper and 'post' it in the appropriate box. Organise four groups and allocate a box to each group. Each group must then sort out the responses and summarise the ideas to present to the rest of the class.

FINDING OUT: SAMPLE ACTIVITIES

PURPOSE
- to further stimulate the students' curiosity
- to provide new information which may answer some of the students' earlier questions
- to raise other questions for the students to explore in the future
- to challenge the students' knowledge, beliefs and values
- to help students to make sense of further activities and experiences which have been planned for them

17 Decision-making in our schools

Find out about the system of leadership and decision-making in the school. Map this out on a large chart. Who is responsible for what? What happens when an important decision needs to be made?

Figure 37 *Children chart the system of decision-making in the school*

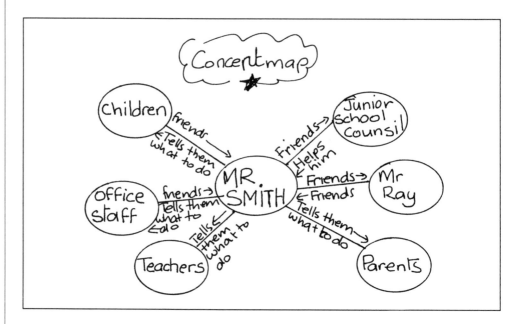

18 Interviews

Interview someone (or a panel of speakers) in a position of leadership who makes decisions that directly affect others. Examples of such people include:

the school principal

president of a school council

member of local or state government

manager of a business

leader of a specific interest/lobby group such as the conservation foundation

Keep a record of the interview such as audio or video tape or notes.

19 Leadership in the local community

Find out about the leaders within the local community. Who are they and for what are they responsible? Contact the local council to seek this information.

20 Case study: Anita Roddick

Use *blackline master 14* to introduce students to someone who has deliberately set about influencing the decisions of others and who has become a 'leader' in a particular field. Having read through the biography, construct a simple profile of Anita Roddick as a rehearsal for the group work on world leaders to follow.

21 Ongoing research task: world leaders

Small groups select a 'world leader' to prepare a profile about. In selecting world leaders, consider those who have deliberately set out to change something, and to influence others in a global sense. There are those who influence people indirectly because they have become famous (e.g. pop stars, actors). The emphasis in this activity is on people whose work is more deliberately and explicitly linked to a recognised leadership role. Some examples of world leaders about whom students may gather information include:

Nelson Mandela

John F Kennedy

Mother Theresa

Benazir Bhutto

Dalai Lama

David Suzuki

Mahatma Ghandi

Queen Elizabeth II

Aung San Suu Kyi

This activity is carried out using a jigsaw grouping strategy (see chapter 3). Small groups (e.g. trios) are responsible for becoming 'experts' on one leader. Once profiles have been completed, individuals from each group form other larger groups within which they will share the information they have gathered.

In many places, excerpts of government processes are televised. Watch a segment of this as a class and analyse the nature and purpose of the work being carried out. What decisions are being explored or made here? Who is involved? How are issues being tackled and resolved?

SORTING OUT: SAMPLE ACTIVITIES

PURPOSE

* to provide students with concrete means of sorting out and representing information and ideas arising from the 'finding out' stage
* to provide students with the opportunity to process the information they have gathered and present this in a number of ways
* to allow for a diverse range of outcomes

23 Working with interview data

The way in which students work with the data gathered from interviews will depend largely on the nature of the data itself. Students themselves can be asked: *What do you think is the best way for us to work with the information we have just heard?* Brainstorm a list of possibilities and allow students to select from this. An example is:

1. Prepare a written dialogue based on the interview.
2. Build a retrieval chart based on the interview.

Listening to Councillor Jones helped us understand	Listening to Councillor Jones made us wonder about ...

3. Create a comic strip or similar illustration of a typical day in the life of the person that you interviewed.
4. Write a letter of thanks to your guest outlining what you learnt.
5. Write a report for the school newsletter or local newspaper summarising the key points gained from the interview.

6. Compare the locals leaders you interviewed with the ideal leaders created earlier in the unit. What characteristics and roles did they share? Would there be anything you would change about your ideal leader? Why?

24 Working with the Anita Roddick case study

Blackline master 14 can be used in many ways. Some issues that might be explored through discussion, art, drama or writing include:

- Courage and risk-taking
- The way in which Anita Roddick was successful on her own
- Anita Roddick made choices and had control over her life. Why? Compare with your own life. What are some of the things you feel passionate about? How could you go about influencing others about this or acting on your beliefs in some way?

25 Looking at the world leader profiles: class discussion

Once students have presented their profiles in groups, conduct a whole class discussion about the patterns and issues arising. Some focus questions could include:

What are some common characteristics of the people we have been researching?
Can you trace any common links in the events that lead to their prominence?
What is it about these people that has made them so influential?
What are the factors that helped and hindered them?
What is the relationship between those who are not part of a formal government and the work of formal governments?

26 Meeting of minds

Divide the class into pairs. Each person will play a character selected from the 'world leaders' list. The combination of characters can be selected according to the focus you wish to explore. You may choose to match a political leader with a community-based leader, a current leader with someone who is no longer alive, or two people who share very different points of view, for example: David Suzuki meets the leader of the country. Students work up a role-play which may then be performed to the class. Ask them to consider the following:

What would they say to each other?
How might David Suzuki wish to influence the president/leader of the country?
What might the president/leader of the country's response to this be?

27 Puppet making

Students make puppets of their leaders and develop short plays depicting the leaders involved in making decisions. The leaders could also interact with each other—hold a world summit!

28 Who am I?

This game can be played at any time during the processing stage of the unit to help revise significant information about the world leaders students have studied and to consider others. Using the profiles as a basis, students devise a list of clues that others use to guess the person, for example:
'Who am I?' games can be played orally and published as a 'guess who' book.

> Who am I?
>
> I was born in South Africa.
>
> I was jailed for many years because of my political beliefs.
>
> I was instrumental in the campaign to end apartheid in South Africa.

29 Working with media watch articles

The articles gathered during the unit can be used in a range of ways. Here are some suggestions:

(a) PNI: Positive, negative, interesting (see chapter 3)

Analyse the issues using De Bono's PNI structure. Select a possible solution to a current political issue. Consider all the **positive** and **negative** aspects of this solution. Now consider those aspects that would be 'interesting to see'.

(b) Classify the articles under various headings.

(c) Use the articles as the basis for DRTA.

(d) Consider this statement: *Political situations arise out of disagreement or conflict.* Do the articles and issues you have been exploring support this idea? What other generalisations can you make?

(e) Examine the structure of a report as used in the newspaper articles. What format do reporters use to construct their pieces? Students write their own reports based on current issues in the school or local community.

(f) Make a timeline of the events that occur as an issue unfolds.

(g) Images of leaders. Look at the way leaders are portrayed in the media (visual, print, radio). View (or listen to) media excerpts.

> *Are the images positive or negative?*
>
> *What kinds of words and visual images are used to describe and portray leaders to the public?*
>
> *What actions and behaviours are selected to be shown to the public via the newspaper and television?*
>
> *Are different leaders portrayed in different ways? Are male leaders portrayed differently from female leaders?*
>
> *What do leaders talk about? What words and phrases are commonly used by leaders? Why?*
>
> *How do leaders present to the public? What clothes do they wear? Are they confident, assertive, aggressive, friendly, persuasive, interested or not interested?*
>
> *Overall, how do people in the community think and feel about leaders?*
>
> *How do images of leaders influence our decision-making?*

GOING FURTHER: SAMPLE ACTIVITIES

PURPOSE

- to extend and challenge students' understanding about the topic
- to provide more information in order to broaden the range of understandings available to the students

30 Excursion to local or state government offices

At this stage in the unit, students should be well prepared to visit their local or state government office. Ideally, arrange to see some work in progress and, if possible, to be given a tour or talk whilst at the venue. Prepare for the visit by examining the drawings/written pieces done earlier in the unit showing students' perceptions of the way their system of government works. Ask them: *What do you expect to see? What questions do you have?*

31 The voice of the people

Examine issues that have motivated people to group together in support for or opposition to decisions made by leaders. Begin by looking at current local and global issues of this nature (e.g. saving a particular area of land), then look back at similar events in history—again at local and global levels. For example: What significant events in our history or world history were a result of people strongly opposing leaders' decisions?—revolutions, uprisings, union movements, blockades, marches, wars, etc.

32 Falling from grace

Examine the balance between leadership and power. Ask students to consider how democracies are designed to ensure this balance is kept. Is it always successful? A focus on world leaders who have misused their leadership, for example Hitler, Pol Pot, and an analysis of the patterns in the histories of these people would also assist this examination.

33 Comparing systems

Have students examine other government systems in other parts of the world and compare and contrast these their own. Develop working definitions of these terms and discuss the following questions:

socialist   democracy   monarchy
communist   autocracy   aristocracy

What is the role of the leader in these systems? What is the role of the 'led'?
How would we describe our classroom/school in the light of these definitions?
Ask students to reflect on the style of leadership in their classroom or school.

MAKING CONNECTIONS: SAMPLE ACTIVITIES

PURPOSE

• For students to draw conclusions about what they have learnt

Return to some of the activities completed in 'tuning in' and 'preparing to find out'. Ask students to reflect on the ways their ideas have changed? Why? What would you say and do differently now?

34 Revisit key words

Give students the key words provided for activity 8. How would they now respond to them? Revisit or re-create concept maps using these key words. What generalisations emerge?

35 What's the link?

In small groups, discuss and record a response to the question:
What is the connection between leadership and decision-making?
This could be represented visually or in written form.

36 Direct analogies

In small groups students brainstorm their responses to some analogies built around the key concepts they have been exploring (see chapter 3):

How is making a decision like juggling?

How is our classroom like parliament?

How is being a leader like bungee jumping?

How is a council meeting like a football game?

How is our society like an ant nest?

Ask students then to devise their own analogies for the same concepts or for others you have explored during the unit. Brainstorm the question: *How is the way our classroom works like that of our system of government? How is it different?*

37 Governing our classroom

Students may be introduced to formal meeting processes by establishing a class meeting time. A formal agenda is devised and worked through each week. Direct students to use what they have learnt about the system of government in their community/state/country to set up a simulation of it in the classroom. This activity can be carried out over a short period or it might be a more elaborate activity that is developed throughout the unit.

TAKING ACTION: SAMPLE ACTIVITIES

PURPOSE

- to assist students to make links between their understandings and their experience in the real world
- to enable students to make choices and develop the belief that they can be effective participants in society

38 Student representative council

Suggest to students that they set up a student representative committee to report to the school council. Issues of concern can be relayed from this committee to the council for discussion and review.

39 Informing others

Students create pamphlets or books to help others understand how to be change agents or decision-makers. This could be done with a specific audience in mind, for example members of the athletics club.

40 Parliament time

A class parliament or class meeting can be conducted in front of parents and friends where students demonstrate their understandings about the formal decision-making process.

41 Decisions for the future

Ask students to consider the things they will need to decide upon in their future. This could be represented on a simple timeline (e.g. what to do when I leave school, where to live).

42 Putting you in the picture

Using the strategy outlined in chapter 3, students reflect on the implications of their learning about decision-making on their own lives. Refer to the section 'Focus on genre: reflection'.

ANITA RODDICK

Anita Roddick was born in England in 1942. Her mother used to say to her: 'Be special, be anything but mediocre.' When she grew up, Anita became a teacher and taught young children for a brief time. She left teaching to travel all around the world, enjoying the freedom, the places she visited and the people she met. When she returned to England, she met her husband Gordon.

Anita and Gordon had two daughters and owned a number of businesses. After some time, Gordon left the family to tour around South America. While he was away, Anita decided that she wanted to open a little shop to sell cosmetics made from natural products, without fancy packaging. At first, the bank would not lend her the money because she was a woman and her husband was away, so a friend gave her some money as a loan to begin the Body Shop. Her business began to do so well that Body Shops opened all over England and then all over the world.

In 1985, she decided that her business had to show that it cared about what was going on in the world. She felt that she could not separate her beliefs about the environment and human suffering from her work. She began to promote the Save the Whale campaign for Greenpeace in her shops. After this, she began to educate the community about the environment, recycling, tests carried out on animals for the cosmetics industry and so on. Messages about these issues were painted on the side of all the delivery trucks for the Body Shop. Anita also wanted the Body Shop to communicate with their staff, customers, the community, the media, and the world. This was done through displays, charts, illustrations, words, images — all designed to tell others about the Body Shop's beliefs and raise awareness in others. She set up a Community Care Department because the Body Shop became so successful all around the world and she wanted to 'give something back to the community'. All over the world, staff in Body Shops were encouraged to do community work such as working with the homeless, the elderly, and planting trees. The Body Shop also developed the idea of 'Trade Not Aid'. This meant that small local industries in underdeveloped countries were set up with the help of the Body Shop. People in these countries could begin to support themselves and not rely on aid from foreign countries.

The Body Shop is a global company with a strong belief in responsibility. Anita Roddick says that it is a multicultural company that cares about the world and the people in it. Her belief is that business can make a contribution to the future of the world and make choices about making profits and having responsibility for others. Anita also argues that it is important to have control over your own life.

(Adapted from *Body and Soul* by Anita Roddick, Vermillion, 1992)

UNIT 6

TOOLS FOR WORK

An integrated unit of work about simple technology and its impact on the way we live for younger students

ABOUT THIS UNIT

This unit is designed to introduce young students to the relationship between work and technology. Implicitly, this unit develops students' understanding of what 'work' is. It encourages students to consider ways in which everyday tasks are made easier by the use of tools, and explores the idea that, as technology changes, so do aspects of the way we live and work.

The unit provides a useful context for the investigation of gender and technology. It challenges views held about the kind of work carried out by men and women and endeavors to promote the notion that all people are capable of working in a range of fields and with a range of tools. Activities help students understand that even very simple household implements are tools and that everyone uses technology in their work. Some simple values clarification activities are included to encourage students to begin thinking critically about the impact of technology on our lives—both positively and negatively.

This is not a unit about the physical science of how tools work . However, it would benefit from being preceded by a such a unit or accompanied by a sequence of experiences focusing on basic mechanics of levels, pulleys, ramps, cogs and wheels, etc.

KEY TERMS

technology	design
needs and wants	materials
work	change

UNDERSTANDINGS AROUND WHICH THE UNIT IS BASED

There are many different kinds of tools and they can be used for many different purposes.

Tools are used in almost everything we do.

Tools allow us to do more than would otherwise be possible.

Technological developments impact on our lives in different ways.

Some technological developments are very simple whilst others are more complex.

Technological developments have changed over time and continue to change.

Products of technology are developed to satisfy needs and wants.

KEY PERSPECTIVES IN SOCIAL EDUCATION

Imagining and constructing the future

Individual potential

Changing lifestyles—work and leisure

Developing values

KEY LEARNING OUTCOMES FOR SOCIAL EDUCATION

Identifies the work done by self and others

Describes the way tools are used in everyday life

Identifies a range of types of work including work done at home

Classifies according to a range of criteria

Justifies views and opinions

Distinguishes between needs and wants

Generates ideas for own designs

Follows steps to acquire information

LANGUAGE OUTCOMES

Uses written and oral language to provide simple explanations

Constructs meaning from visual texts

Uses specialised terms in conjunction with conceptual understandings about tools

Frames a simple question for inquiry

Uses language (oral, written and symbolic) to reflect on learning

SELECTION OF TEXTS

You will need to consider the range of texts (written, spoken and visual) needed to help students to access information about tools. Some of these could include photographs, discussions with guest speakers and instruction manuals.

DEVELOPING A CRITICAL PERSPECTIVE

As this unit of work involves students in the use of a wide range of texts such as those listed above, it is essential that students consider the authenticity of these texts and the reliability of the data, and read these texts with a critical perspective. Particular attention should be given to the images associated with tools—are they inclusive in that they show people of different gender, age and ethnic backgrounds using these tools?

Focus on genre: explanation

This unit requires students to develop understandings about tools—what they are used for and who uses them. It therefore lends itself well to the explicit teaching of the genre of explanation. The explicit teaching of this genre provides students with greater control over the genres and will add to their repertoire of oral and written language skills. This focus on genre is a 'unit within a unit' and we suggest you take time from the unit of work to focus on the modelling and application of the genre.

KEY FEATURES OF THE EXPLANATION GENRE

Purpose: An explanation provides an account of how something works or why a particular phenomenon is how it is.

Structure: An explanation begins with a **statement** about the particular phenomenon, for example:

Scissors are used to cut things.

and this is followed by an **explanation** of how/why something occurs or how something works:

Scissors have two sharp blades and handles for you to grip.

Language used: Usually the features of an explanation are non-human:

Some scissors are used in the kitchen.

and there are words that signal a time relationship:

After the handle of the scissors are gripped

and cause and effect relationships:

If the scissors are not held correctly, then ...

Action verbs (*cuts, separates*) as well as some passive verbs (*is, held*) are used, as is the timeless present tense (*are, kept, needed, is*).

TEACHING SEQUENCE: EXPLANATIONS

The following shows *one approach* to teaching key features of the information genre. For more detailed advice refer to Derewianka (1990) and Wing Jan (1991).

Teacher modelling: A range of models of explanations (written and oral) can be used. Explanations which outline the use of tools in the classroom or in the home, for example instruction manuals, would be suitable. These explanations allow students to access information, and also work as models for their own written or oral explanation. You could create an explanation to use to model and demonstrate the key features of the genre to your students.

Spotlight on structure: The structure of an explanation relates to the purpose of the text and its intended audience. Questioning students about the structure of the text allows them to focus on the particular structure of this genre and apply this to their own written or oral language.

How does the explanation begin?

Are the explanations of how something works made clear? Do you understand what it is telling you?

Spotlight on language features: Language used in an explanation helps to create the particular meaning of the text. A focus on how the language used creates meaning enables students to choose language appropriate to this genre in their own written or oral language.

What tense has been used? Are there any action verbs?

Have linking words to do with a time sequence been used?

Other things to consider:

Have you been able to find out how something works?

Have you been able to include relevant information to your audience?

Will your audience understand your information?

Is your information accurate?

Have you included the most important facts and information?

PREPARATION

- Begin collecting a range of examples of simple tools that do a variety of jobs, for example:

scissors	can opener	sharpener
pizza cutter	garlic crusher	hand beater
hand drill	hammer	screwdriver
stapler	pen	knitting needles
stitch unpicker		

- Collect old parts and junk materials students could use to construct tools.
- Write to parents and ask if they would contribute old tools and implements that could be used during the unit
- Gather together a collection of factual texts about tools.
- Arrange visits by guest speakers from various occupations—demonstrating both men and women in a range of occupations, or arrange a visit to a work place to look at people using tools in various ways.
- Gather images (pictures, posters, etc) of people at work using a variety of tools.

TUNING IN: SAMPLE ACTIVITIES

PURPOSE

- to provide students with opportunities to become engaged with the topic
- to ascertain the students' initial curiosity about the topic
- to allow students to share their personal experience of the topic

1 What's in the bag?

Place a tool in a bag or box. Tell students they must guess what is in the bag but their questions will only receive a yes or no response. (Examples: Is it made of wood? Does it have moving parts? Would you find it in the kitchen?) Once they have practised the questioning technique, students take turns to put tools in the bag and be questioned by others. The same activity can be done using a feely box strategy. The item is placed in a box or bag and students must guess what it is by feeling it. (NB This alternative should only be used with tools that are safe to handle.)

2 Play and exploration

Set up an area in the classroom where students can work with tools in an informal way. Allow time each day for a small group of students to 'play' with the tools and to talk to each other about what the tools are used for. Also make available construction equipment such as Lego or Duplo and ask students to add to the table any tools they make themselves.

3 Collecting tools

Ask students to bring tools and implements from home and add to a display area. They could share their particular item at morning news time and explain how it is used in their home.

PREPARING TO FIND OUT: SAMPLE ACTIVITIES

PURPOSE

- to find out what the students already know about the topic
- to provide the students with a focus for the forthcoming experience
- to help in the planning of further experiences and activities

4 Brainstorm: murals

Explain to students that tools are items we use to help us work — to help us get jobs done. In small groups, students then brainstorm all the tools they can think of that belong:

in the classroom

in our homes

in the school and school grounds

Ideas can be recorded in words or pictures and added to using images from magazines, newspapers, shopping catalogues, etc. These brainstorms should be revisited, added to and modified throughout the unit.

5 Classifying tools

Ask students to put a collection of tools into groups that they think belong together. They then think of a label for their categories. In groups, students could make a collection for which others have to guess their grouping criteria, for example: 'A group where all tools are made of metal' or 'A group where all tools are used in the classroom'.

6 A world of work

Make a class list of all the different types of work that students can think of, such as: housework, gardening, school work, looking after babies, office work. Divide the class into trios and assign one type of work to each. They must brainstorm all the different tools that help people carry out that work.

7 Statements and questions

Ask students:

What do we know about the way tools help us?

What questions do we have about how tools help us?

Encourage students to record their ideas individually and then share these with the class. A group list of statements and questions should be compiled and displayed for reference throughout the unit.

8 Mimes

Students mime the use of a particular tool and other class members must guess what they are 'using' (for example: opening a can; hammering a nail). This same activity can be done in small groups using a more complex form of movement and mime. Ask students to think of a particular tool and to become the tool as a group. Again, others must guess what they are showing.

9 How do we use tools every day?

In small groups, students are given a card with a common, daily task written or drawn on it, such as:

Making a sandwich

Eating breakfast

Having a bath/shower

Students then brainstorm all the tools that are used to help complete the activity—in words or pictures. This could be done using a sequential comic strip representation of the activity, from beginning to end. Share and display students' work. Make a list of all the tools shown in their drawings.

Begin a simple data chart on the wall. This can be added to throughout the unit.

Name of tool	What do we use it for?

10 In the kitchen

Ask students to close their eyes and try to visualise all the tools used to do things in the kitchen. They then draw their kitchen and show these items. This could also be done using models and could be extended to other rooms in the house.

Students then share their drawing with someone else and note the things that are the same and the things that are different.

Pairs join and make a list of all the things that are the same.

Share as a class: *What are the common tools in our kitchens? What things are different? Why?* Students then take drawings home and add to their pictures and their lists.

11 Magazine hunt

Using old magazines, students cut out pictures of tools that help people do things. Paste the pictures onto cards and use them as the basis for:

classifying

lucky dip games

ordering (biggest to smallest, different rooms, most to least important, easy to use to hard to use, etc.)

12 Who uses what?

Provide students with **blackline master 15** showing pictures of different people in different occupations. They then draw the tools they think would be needed by those people. Share and discuss.

13 Initial generalisations

Now make a class list of statements about tools and work. Individual students contribute a statement to the list. Record their name alongside the statement to allow future reference and modification.

FINDING OUT: SAMPLE ACTIVITIES

PURPOSE

- to further stimulate the students' curiosity
- to provide new information which may answer some of the students' earlier questions
- to raise other questions for students to explore in the future
- to challenge the students' knowledge, beliefs and values
- to help students to make sense of further activities and experiences which have been planned for them

14 Tools around the house

Students make a list of tools that are used in and around the home. These are compiled onto a large class list and classified.

15 Tools at work: survey

Design a simple set of questions students could use to interview their parents about the tools used in their work. Questions should gather information about the uses and types of tools.

16 Guest speakers

Invite several guest speakers in to show the students the way they use tools in their work. These people could be drawn from the school community itself. Set up small 'work stations' with a guest speaker at each, around which small groups of students rotate. This provides students with more opportunity for hands-on experience with the tools the guest has brought in, and a chance to ask more questions than in a large group situation. Ensure that the group of people invited is inclusive in terms of both gender and types of occupation.

17 Excursion: tools in action

Conduct an excursion to a place where a range of tools are used such as a building site or factory.

18 Local walk

Walk around the local area with students and observe the way people use tools in their everyday lives. Keep a photographic record of your observations.

19 Past and present

Changing technology can be well illustrated by showing students examples of tools of the past. Invite an older person in to discuss and show examples of tools they used in the past. It may also be possible to visit a museum where such tools might be on display, or to build up a collection in the classroom. Students could try to predict, first, how people used to perform the same task they do now without the modern implement, for example:

mincer—replaced by food processor
washboard—replaced by washing machine
hand mower—replaced by electric mower
box camera—replaced by instamatic camera
typewriter—replaced by word processor
fire-heated iron—replaced by electric iron

When showing students these tools, ask them:

Who has seen one of these before? Where?
What do you know about it?
What do you think this was used for?
What do we do now?
How are the old and new items different?
Which one would you prefer to use? Why?
What might be the good things about the older item?

What might be the negative things about it?

How did it work?

What kind of energy did it require?

Give students the experience of actually using the older equipment to complete a task. (e.g. make butter from cream by using a hand-beater) and ask them to talk about the difference in effort, results, etc.

SORTING OUT: SAMPLE ACTIVITIES

PURPOSE

- to provide students with concrete means of sorting out and representing information and ideas arising from the 'finding out' stage
- to provide students with the opportunity to process the information they have gathered and present this in a number of ways
- to allow for a diverse range of outcomes

20 Ongoing data chart

As information from parents and friends is gathered, students record it onto personal or class data charts.

Occupation	What kind of work is done?	What tools are needed?

21 Tools around the home: models and dioramas

As students gather information about tools used around the home, this can be represented on a large model. The construction of the model should, itself, involve tools (scissors, brushes, modelling tools, etc.). Use Lego to construct a house and make small replicas of tools (using modelling clay) to place around the house. Alternatively, students could make dioramas using old shoe boxes. Inside the box, represent one room of the house, showing all the places where tools can be found. Students can then write an explanation of how a particular tool works.

22 A day in the life of ...

Using the information gained by the panel of different occupations, students devise short scenes from a day in the life of a builder/vet/machinist/gardener, etc. These scenes could be represented through role-play, art or simple explanations.

23 Graph

Combine results of the survey about tools at work (activity 15) and visually represent these on a large graph. Ask students: *What tools are used most often in work? Why? What tools are used least often? Who uses the tools? Why?*

GOING FURTHER: SAMPLE ACTIVITIES

PURPOSE

- to extend and challenge students' understanding about the topic
- to provide for more information in order to broaden the range of understandings available to the students

24 Tools in other cultures

Examine picture sets, videos or books that depict people from another culture using different tools to help their work. Show students, for example, ways in which natural materials are modified and used as tools by some traditional indigenous people to prepare and cook food, build homes, etc. A simple contrast could be made across cultures of the different tools used in preparing and eating food. Encourage students to consider the reasons for these differences and the advantages and disadvantages they see of using the different tools.

25 Do we really need it?

From the various lists and pictures of tools around the room, ask students to classify those which people *need* and those that people *want*. There will be discussion and disagreement about what constitutes a need; allow this to arise and for students to explore the concept. Ask students to think about the tools they have around the home—which of those could they do without?

26 Desert island dilemma

Students imagine that they have been marooned on a desert island. Ask them to choose five tools that would help them survive. They draw and write about their choice and then share their ideas with others.

27 Imagine a world without ...

Present pairs of students with a hypothetical situation in which a particular tool no longer exists and alternatives must be found. Some examples are:

Imagine life without toothbrushes
Imagine life without knives and forks
Imagine life without scissors
Imagine life without brushes and combs

In pairs, students discuss what would happen in this situation and the alternatives they could use. Compile the ideas into a class book.

MAKING CONNECTIONS: SAMPLE ACTIVITIES

PURPOSE

- for students to draw conclusions about what they have learnt
- to provide students with opportunities for reflection both on what has been learnt and on the learning process

28 How important are they?

Provide students with a list of common tools (those that they are now familiar with). These can be put on cards and ordered from most to least important.

You could begin by asking students to nominate the most important tool from the list and to say why. Other students could order the entire list.

Students then do the same thing but from the perspective of various people in a range of occupations, for example a teacher, a baby, a builder, a chef.

29 Laying it on the line

Using the strategy outlined in chapter 3, present students with a series of controversial statements about tools based on the work you have carried out so far. They must decide on the extent to which they agree or disagree with the statements and justify their ideas. Sample statements:

Men need to use tools more than women in their work

Modern tools are better than old fashioned tools

We can survive without tools

Only adults use tools

30 Review and restate

Students return to the lists, pictures, questions, etc. generated at the beginning of the unit. Ask them: *How have your ideas changed? What do you know now that you didn't know then?* Students reflect on this in their learning logs.

31 Statements of generalisation

Use **blackline master 16** to provide students with a structured format for making conclusions about the topic. Some students may need you to act as scribe for their ideas.

32 Concept mapping

Students demonstrate their understandings about tools by mapping the connections between key words about the topic. The words may be generated by individuals or selected from the words around the room. Students share maps with each other.

Figure 38 *Students have a framework for making conclusions about the topic*

① People use lots of tools at work becose they need to do their work.

② Tools are used to help people at work at home on out side

③ Some tools are hard to use at work and some tools have elictric. Some tools have levers.

④ Some tools have changed into old tools and some tools don't work when they are old.

⑤ I can use many tools like scissors, can openers like mum and dad.

33 Theatre sports

Using the collection of implements in the classroom, give individuals or pairs two or three tools and ask them to come up with a simple scenario in which all the tools are used in some way.

TAKING ACTION: SAMPLE ACTIVITIES

PURPOSE

- to assist students to make links between their understandings and their experience in the real world
- to enable students to make choices and develop the belief that they can be effective participants in society
- to provide further insight into students' understandings for future unit planning

34 Designing a new tool

Present students with simple, everyday tasks. They must design a tool that would make the task easier. Some examples include:

Picking up papers in the school grounds

Making a cubby house

Changing a baby's nappy

Sorting rubbish for recycling

Feeding the dog

35 Fixing up the classroom

Present students with a simple problem in the classroom and work out a plan to solve it, for example:

Something is broken

There are staples in the notice board

The window won't close properly

Ask students:

How can we solve this problem?

What tools will we need?

Carry out the task.

WHO USES WHAT?

Draw the tools these people might need in their work.

Dentist

Parent

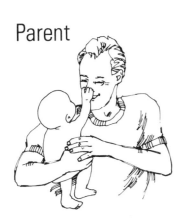

Teacher

Chef

Farmer

Builder

WHAT DO YOU KNOW?

Write your ideas in a sentence.

1 People and tools

2 What tools are used for

3 Types of tools

4 How tools have changed

5 You and tools

UNIT 7

TRADING PLACES

A unit of work about trade and international relations for upper primary

ABOUT THIS UNIT

The focus of this unit is on trade between countries and the ways in which trade can work to secure or weaken relationships between countries. The unit is designed to help students to discover ways in which international trade helps satisfy needs and wants at the local level, as well as developing understandings about the global network of relationships established around trade agreements. Importantly, activities in the unit take students from a basic understanding of trade as the exchange of goods and services through to an appreciation of the complex systems of domination and influence which are established through the delicate balance between trade relationships; how some countries remain powerful at the expense of others.

Through this unit, students not only learn about international trade but develop an understanding of the broad concept of a fair partnership. The topic also provides students with an insight into the interdependent global community in which they live.

KEY TERMS

trade	exchange	market
economy	import	export
embargo	agreement	trade
surplus	profit	partnership
systems	relationships	needs and wants
power and control		

UNDERSTANDINGS AROUND WHICH THIS UNIT IS BASED

There is a network of interdependence between people in countries around the world.

All people have needs and wants.

Some of these needs and wants are satisfied at a local level but many are satisfied through international trade.

Trade involves the exchange of goods and services between and within countries to satisfy needs and wants.

Countries form trade agreements with each other in order to export and import services for mutual benefit.

There are systems and structures to establish and assist trade agreements between countries.

Trading relationships may be used by some countries to exert power and influence over others.

Trading relationships between countries may change over time. These changes occur for a range of reasons.

KEY PERSPECTIVES IN SOCIAL EDUCATION

The global society
Developing values
Thinking critically
Justice, rights and responsibilities

KEY LEARNING AREAS FOR SOCIAL EDUCATION

Identifies the decisions involved in satisfying needs and wants

Explains features of international trade and how they impact at the local level

Portrays aspects of international relations from different perspectives

Conveys the network of relationships established through trade

Analyses trade relationships in terms of the systems of power established

LANGUAGE OUTCOMES

Uses written and oral language for reporting information

Expresses and justifies a point of view

Uses specialised terms in conjunction with conceptual understandings about trade

SELECTION OF TEXTS

You will need to consider the range of texts (written, spoken and visual) needed to help students to access information about international trade. Some of these texts could include maps, dictionaries, statistical information, discussions with guest speakers, written information from consulates and embassies, newspaper reports and so on.

DEVELOPING A CRITICAL PERSPECTIVE

As this unit of work involves students in the use of a wide range of texts such as those listed above, it is essential that they consider the authenticity of these texts and the reliability of the data, and so read these texts with a critical perspective.

Focus on genre: information report

This unit requires students to develop understandings about international trade. It therefore lends itself well to the explicit teaching of the information report genre, thereby allowing students to use reports for accessing information and experience and as models for the creation of written and oral reports to process their understandings. The explicit teaching of reports provides students with greater control over this genre and will add to their repertoire of oral and written language skills. This focus on genre is a 'unit within a unit' and we suggest you take time from the unit of work to focus on the modelling and application of the genre.

KEY FEATURES OF INFORMATION REPORT GENRE

Purpose: An information report outlines or provides information on a particular topic.

Structure: An information report begins with a **classification**, for example:

Vietnam is located in South-East Asia.

and the rest of the report consists of facts about the subject, for example:

Vietnam exports oil, rice, coffee, tea, textiles and clothing and seafood.

Language used: Usually the items referred to in a report are generalised, for example *trading partners, goods and services*. There is some use of action verbs *(trade)* and the timeless present tense is used (*Much of the country is covered in forest and there are huge river networks which run through the country*). There are linking verbs such as *are* and *is* and reference to technical terms, for example: *In recent years, Vietnam's economy has begun to improve. In 1992 it achieved a small trade surplus.* The language of the information report is formal and objective so there is no reference to opinion or emotion. Instead, language is used for classifying, comparing and contrasting: *Vietnam's major trading partners are Singapore, Japan, Hong Kong, Taiwan, France and the Republic of Korea.*

TEACHING SEQUENCE: INFORMATION REPORTS

The following shows *one approach* to teaching key features of the information genre. For more detailed advice refer to Derewianka (1990) and Wing Jan (1991).

Teacher modelling: A range of models of information report writing and oral language can be used. Reports which outline factual information about a country or an item that is traded would be suitable. These reports allow students to access information, and also work as models for their own writing or oral reporting. You could create an information report to use to model and demonstrate the key features of the genre to your students.

Spotlight on structure: The structure of an information report relates to the purpose of the text and its intended audience. Questioning students about the structure of the text allows them to focus on the particular features of this genre and to apply these to their own written or oral language.

> *How is the written/oral report structured?*
> *Does the report begin with a classification?*
> *Are facts included?*

Spotlight on language features: Language used in an information report helps to create the particular meaning of the text. A focus on how the language is used to create meaning enables students to choose language appropriate to this genre in their own written/oral language.

> *What words sentences/phrases are used?*
> *What is included and what is left out?*
> *Have technical terms been used?*
> *Have the technical terms been explained?*

Other things to consider:

> *Have you been able to include information relevant to your audience?*
> *Will your audience understand your information?*
> *Is your information accurate?*
> *Have you included the most important facts and information?*
> *Have you used technical terms?*
> *Have you explained the technical terms?*

PREPRATION

- Organise learning logs for each child (see chapter 3).
- Collect examples of imported items.
- Consider guest speakers for 'finding out'.
- Begin collecting relevant newspaper and magazine articles relating to international trade.
- Design a draft research contract (see chapter 3).

TUNING IN: SAMPLE ACTIVITIES

PURPOSE

- to provide students with opportunities to become engaged with the topic
- to ascertain the students' initial curiosity in the topic
- to allow students to begin to share their personal experience of the topic

1 Fair trade

Begin the unit by asking students to bring an item from home that they would be prepared to exchange for something else. What follows is a hypothetical exchange. Students will take their own item home at the end of the activity.

1. Students bring an item from home that they would be (hypothetically) willing to exchange for other items
2. Display items and allow students to peruse the collection
3. Students individually make a list of those items that they would like to exchange with their own, then share lists
4. Individuals consider those items that would be a fair exchange, then share ideas
5. As a class, discuss the criteria used to decide what constitutes a fair exchange

2 Discussion: What do we collect and trade?

As a class, students discuss the things they commonly exchange, for example in the playground, after school, during sporting activities, at home. Some students or their parents may belong to clubs where such exchanges are formalised: stamp collections, cards, vintage car clubs, etc. Students could then bring their collections to school and explain why they collect the item and the trades/exchanges they have made.

PREPARING TO FIND OUT: SAMPLE ACTIVITIES

PURPOSE

- to find out what the students already know about the topic
- to provide the students with a focus for the forthcoming experience
- to help in the planning of further experiences and activities

3 Word association

Individually or in groups, students brainstorm ideas around these key words: trade, exchange, market, economy, import, export, World Bank. *What do you think of when you read/hear these words?*

Responses can be shared and pasted in learning logs for later reference. Throughout the unit students should be encouraged to revisit their initial ideas and add, modify, change or reject them.

4 How did it get here?

Bring an imported item such as a pair of sports shoes, food, a kitchen appliance, a walkman, into the classroom and ask students questions such as the following:

I bought this cassette player at a local shop, but it has a 'Made in Taiwan' label on it. Why do you think that is so? How do you think it came to be in our local store? Why is it there?

This is followed by a whole class brainstorm of ideas about the journey and events and decisions that might have taken place to get the item here.

Individually, students then make a list of items in their home that they think are made in another country. Follow this with a list of those that they think are made in their own country. These lists could also be used to classify under the headings: *needs* and *wants*. If necessary, time can be spent clarifying the distinction between the two.

At home, students check/confirm/add to their lists. Ask each student to bring to school one suitable item made in another country. Share and discuss.

5 Group problem-solving

Using the items brought from home, students work in small groups to visually map the journey of events (this could be drawn, labelled, written, diagrammatic, or a combination of these) that might have taken place to get the item here. Groups now share their drawings and diagrams. Ask them:

What do all of these diagrams have in common?

What are you saying about how these items got from their country of origin to your homes?

What questions do you have about the journey?

6 Listing key questions

List key questions arising from the group problem-solving activity on a chart with students' names attached to them. These can be used as a reference throughout the unit and in reflection and summary at the end.

7 Hypothesising

Students now return to groups and hypothesise as to *why* the item came from another country in the first place. Various reasons are written on strips and classified under headings, for example: economic reasons, natural resource availability.

In pulling this information together, introduce the terms **export** and **import** and discuss their meanings.

Figure 39 *Students map the journey taken by an imported item from home*

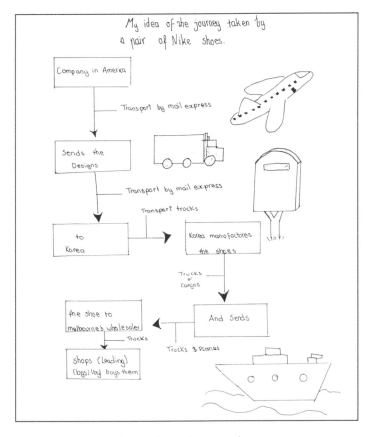

8 Magazine search and collage

Using old magazines, shopping catalogues, newspapers, etc., students cut out pictures of items they think are produced in their own country. Ask:

Which of these items do you think might be wanted and needed by people in other countries? Why?

Which items do you think are, in fact, exported to other countries?

How do you know?

The pictures can then be pasted onto a large collage with students' ideas about satisfying needs and wants written around it.

Figure 40 *Students create a collage to show their ideas*

9 Mapping understandings

Provide students with a simple map of the world such as the one on **Blackline master 17**. In pairs, students label the countries they know and then hypothesise about the kinds of goods each country might produce. Once these are shared, ask students to circle or color those countries that they think trade with their home country. Use atlases to confirm and add to maps.

(Note that atlases do not always reflect the current shifts in political boundaries and name changes of countries. Students can compare and contrast representations and discuss the reasons behind differences.)

Alternatively, groups of students could be given one major continent, then come together to construct a large map on the classroom wall.

These maps can be kept for the purpose of comparison and assessment later in the unit.

10 Role-play: What do we know about international trade?

Organise students into groups of four—constituting two pairs.
Each group is given two items—one per pair.
Each pair represents the country of origin of their particular item.
Ask the students: *What do you think happens when countries decide to trade goods with each other?*

Pairs must then develop a short dialogue demonstrating the ways they think the items might be traded or exchanged. They then act these exchanges out in front of the rest of the class. Note that teacher guidance is minimal as the emphasis is on assessing students' prior knowledge in the area.

As students perform their dialogues, ask others to observe *what* is talked about and what is done during the role-plays. The following focus questions can be used to guide their observations:

How do they communicate?

Do they come to an agreement? How?

Do they make a record of their deal?

Do they shake hands?

Do they seem happy about the agreement?

Is there a contract or formal agreement between them?

Repeat the dialogues and now ask students to focus on the nature of the language used, for example:

Did they use body language? If so how?

What words did they use? Tone of voice?

What did they need to do to be persuasive?

What did they do with the other person's response?

Discuss with students: *In what other situations have you noticed people using this kind of persuasive talk? In what situations do you use it?* For example, swapping basketball cards, negotiating something with parents or siblings, when you want something, etc. These situations could also be role-played and comparisons made between the two.

11 Learning log entry

Students individually respond to the following questions in their learning logs. They may also reflect on the role-play experience. These logs will be used to record students' reflections on their learning and on the unit itself and should be used regularly. Focus questions for initial entries in learning logs include:

What do you think about international trade?
What do you think about the way countries trade goods?
What questions do you have?

12 Questions for a guest speaker

Using a 1-3-6 consensus strategy (see chapter 3), students come up with a list of questions they would ask someone who was involved in importing or exporting products to or from another country and the particular things of interest they wish to find out.

FINDING OUT: SAMPLE ACTIVITIES

PURPOSE

- further stimulate the students' curiosity
- to provide new information which may answer some of the students' earlier questions
- to raise other questions for the students to explore in the future
- to challenge the students' knowledge, beliefs and values
- to help students to make sense of further activities and experiences which have been planned for them

13 International trade data chart

The data chart provided on **blackline master 19** provides an initial source of information about trade. Whilst the data itself may have changed since publication, it can be used as an example or case study or, alternatively, can be updated before use. A range of activities below are designed to help students to work with the data provided:

1. Give students a copy of the chart with some information boxes covered or whited out. Ask students to hypothesise about the information that could be in those boxes then check their responses against the chart for confirmation.
2. Use the blank boxes provided to add information about additional countries
3. Use a selection of focus questions to help students to understand the information:
   Which countries appear to be the main trading partners?
   Why do you think some of the figures are a number of years old?
   What may have happened between then and now?
   Why are the figures calculated in US dollars?

From the list provided, which countries appear to export more than they import? What do you think would be the implications of this?

14 Setting up research groups

Organise students into small groups (e.g. trios). Using the data chart as a basis, assign a country to each group. The group will have the responsibility of gathering further information about their country and its trade to share with the class later in the unit (see chapter 3). Students may structure their research into a written or oral report (see 'Focus on genre: information reports'). Negotiate a set of questions and tasks for research, such as those below. This will be an *ongoing* activity that prepares students for the final simulation game at the unit's conclusion. It is suggested that you model or demonstrate the task with the whole class using a particular country as an example. Students may then use the following as a guide for their own research:

1. Develop a profile of your country. Example: Australia

> **Geographical location**: Asia-Pacific region, southern hemisphere
> **Population**: 17,000,000 +
> **Climate**: tropical, sub-tropical, temperate and arid
> **Major cities**: Sydney, Melbourne, Perth, Brisbane, Adelaide, Hobart, Darwin
> **Capital city**: Canberra
> **Major industries**: mining, steel manufacture
> **Agriculture**: wheat, sugar, wool, beef
> **Natural resources**: iron ore, bauxite, gold, uranium
> **Level of development**: modern

2. Show on a world map the main trading routes between your country and its trading partners.
3. Find out more about the products imported to your country. Where do they come from? Why might these products be needed by people in your country?
4. Find out about products exported from your country. Where do they go? Why might people in these countries want them?
5. Calculate the difference between the value of the imports and exports (this could be done using the information on the data chart).
6. Calculate whether your country makes a profit from trade.

15 Interview local importer/exporter

Invite someone to speak to the class who is involved in importing or exporting a product. It would be best to invite someone who is involved in a fairly small-scale business so that the information is more simple and accessible to students. Parents in the school community could be a good starting point. Also try local businesses in the area. The questions developed in preparing to 'find out' can be used as a basis for a class interview.

16 Gathering information from larger companies

Contact larger organisations involved in exporting their products to other countries. Many companies produce material to promote their products overseas and employ an education officer for this purpose. Involve students in writing letters to find out what these companies export, where they export to and how they promote their products. Examine material received from companies (e.g. pamphlets, promotional videos, posters). Focus not only on the nature of the product and the concept of export, but also on the way in which the product is promoted.

17 Newspaper search

Begin a bulletin board displaying relevant articles from the newspaper. Encourage students to look at the financial section of the newspaper and to hypothesise about the meaning of some of the reports, for example: *Why do newspapers report the value of the dollar each day? What does this mean?*

SORTING OUT: SAMPLE ACTIVITIES

PURPOSE

- to provide students with concrete means of sorting out and representing information and ideas arising from the 'finding out' stage
- to provide students with the opportunity to process the information they have gathered and present this in a number of ways
- to allow for a diverse range of outcomes

18 Using mathematics to process the information in the data chart

Once students have an understanding of the general nature of the information represented in the data chart, mathematics can be used to explore it in more depth. The following activities are suggested. Before working mathematically with some of the data gathered, it is advisable that time be spent on helping the students to understand the notion of exchange rates and conversion from one monetary system to another. Collect samples of money from different countries and demonstrate the comparative worth of each one, etc.

- Order the countries from the highest to the lowest import dollars. (Have students make predictions first.)
- Put this information onto a graph: What does it tell you? Why?
- Using the current rate of exchange, convert the US dollars into Australian dollars. How does this change your understanding of the information presented?

• Which countries export more than they import? What implications does this have? Introduce the concept of 'trade surplus' and 'trade deficit'.

19 Responding to interviews

Once students have interviewed the local exporter/importer, ask them to reflect in their learning logs under these headings:

What I expected to hear

What I learnt

What I'd still like to know

Using this information gathered from the interview with the local exporter or importer, students visually represent some of the key processes they have learnt about. This could be done using:

comic strips

wall charts

drama

diagrams

report writing (see 'Focus on genre: information report')

20 Processing newspaper reports

Articles gathered from the newspaper can be processed in a range of ways. Select key articles and ask students to identify the main points and summarise the information for others. Provide regular focus questions:

What are these newspaper articles telling us about trade?

What language are they using to talk about trade?

GOING FURTHER: SAMPLE ACTIVITIES

PURPOSE

• to extend and challenge students' understandings about the topic

• to provide more information in order to broaden the range of understandings available to the students

21 Case study of Vietnam

This activity involves students gathering information about international trade with Vietnam through reading a report (see **blackline master 18**).

Preparing to read: possible sentences

To help students prepare for and understand the text on initial reading, use the 'possible sentences' strategy (see chapter 3). Key words which can be used as the focus for possible sentences include:

population	war	trade embargo
debt	trade agreement	World Bank
trade surplus	profit	trading partners
import	export	

Ensure that students are aware that the passage is a **report** about Vietnam and trade before they begin devising their possible sentences. Revise the features of a report (see 'Focus on genre: information report') and emphasise that the text contains factual information about Vietnam and trade.

Figure 41 *Students' work is displayed and shared*

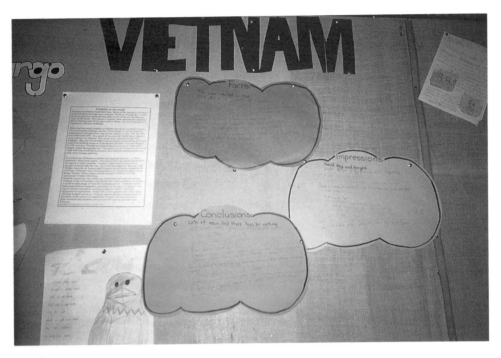

Understanding the text

Use a 3-level guide (see chapter 3) to help students explore and process the content.

Exploring the issues

The following questions will enable the students to develop further understandings about the nature of trade and international relationships:

> *Do you know of any other countries on which a trade embargo or trade 'sanctions' have been imposed or threatened? (E.g. South Africa, Republic of North Korea, Iraq, Serbia)*

> *Why are embargoes or sanctions used? What do you think are the long-term effects of these actions?*

22 Using De Bono's thinking hats

Now students should be ready to explore the issue of trade embargoes in more depth using De Bono's 6 thinking hats (see chapter 3). Divide the class into five groups, each with a different hat. The groups discuss and document the issues according to their given perspectives and come together at the end to share their ideas. (The blue hat is used in a separate activity.)

White: List the facts that you know about trade embargoes (use either the case study of Vietnam or treat the topic more generally).

Red: What are the feelings and emotions associated with this issue? How do you feel? How do you think the people in the affected countries would feel (e.g. Vietnamese people). How do you think the people in the country imposing the embargo would feel?

Black: What are some negative aspects and outcomes of trade embargoes or sanctions?

Yellow: What are some positive aspects and outcomes of trade embargoes or sanctions?

Green: How could the problems leading to embargoes/sanctions be solved in other ways? What could be done instead?

23 Watch this space

As the case study outlines, both the USA and Australia were involved in the war against Vietnam. After the war ended in 1973, Australia initiated diplomatic relations with Vietnam and recognised the new government.

Discuss the differences between Australia's way of ending the conflict with Vietnam and the actions of the United States. Encourage students to voice/ express their opinions about such actions. Consider the long-term implications for Vietnam, Australia and the United States of America.

24 Trading for land

Involve students in finding out about the 'trading' that took place between colonial powers and indigenous peoples. There are numerous examples of the way land was acquired from indigenous people through trade. What implications did the introduction of trade have on the indigenous groups? Find out about 'trade' between indigenous cultures prior to colonisation.

MAKING CONNECTIONS: SAMPLE ACTIVITIES

PURPOSE

* to assist students to draw conclusions and make generalisations about what they have learnt
* to provide opportunities for reflection on both what has been learnt and on the learning process itself

25 Revisit world maps

Repeat activity 9. Students compare their two maps and reflect on what they have learnt so far in the unit.

26 Effects wheels

Consider all the possible effects that arise from the 'opening up' of trade in places that have been closed to much international trade, e.g. Vietnam. Students work in pairs to construct an effects wheel (see chapter 3).
Ask students: *What generalisations can we make, based on our effects wheel?*
Effects wheels could also be made for the following situations:
Rapid development of a country's economy
War (look at effects on trade)
Recessions (in one or other trading partner's country)
Reduced quality of goods being traded (e.g. sheep from Australia to Iraq being diseased)
Crop failures in one or other country

27 Blue-hat thinking

Once students have explored the issue using the five colors, the whole class can come together and discuss the issue from the perspective of the 'blue hat'. This hat encourages the learner to consider the big picture. For example, embargoes can be seen as more than just trade sanctions; they may represent one country exerting their power over another.

What is a 'trade embargo' really all about?

What are the 'big issues'? (e.g. power, punishment, prevention against escalating conflict)

28 Reporting on research: focus on genre — report

Having gathered and collated data about individual countries and trading relationships, and as preparation for the World Fair, students present a written or oral report to share with the class. Reference to the section 'Focus on genre: information report' will help you to assist students discover the key features of a report.

29 Simulation game: World Trade Fair

The purpose of this activity is to allow students to put into practice their understandings about trade.

You will need:

- **Small groups:** Students form small groups of pairs or trios. Each group represents a particular country, preferably a country investigated in research teams earlier in the unit. One group will represent the World Bank.
- **Money:** 'Money' will be required for all countries participating and a fixed currency will need to be agreed upon, for example, US dollars. (NOTE: Countries do not have *equal* amounts of money and the amount can be calculated on the basis of trade figures.) You may, for example, use Monopoly money but allocate a smaller amount to developing countries and large amounts to developed countries. The World Bank is given a fixed amount of money to lend to countries. The group assigned to the World Bank may fix borrowing limits and establish rules for borrowing.
- **Posters:** Students prepare posters to advertise the products their country has to trade.
- **Room or space:** Allocate a space big enough for the World Fair. Students may wish to invite guests in to observe the trading. Each country is assigned a table or booth at which to conduct their negotiations.

Procedure:

1. Each country sets up their stall at the World Fair and advertises the products they have to trade. They may even wish to make examples/ models of the products they will trade with others based on the research conducted earlier in the unit.
2. Each country receives an allotment of money. This allotment can be worked out by the teacher, but needs to represent the unequal distribution of power among trading nations. For example the USA will have more money to trade with than Zimbabwe (use examples from **blackline master 19** to get this information).
3. Each country may approach the World Bank to borrow money. Rules for

borrowing and paying back money need to be established prior to the commencement of the World Fair and made clear to all participants.

4. Free trading is allowed for a given period of time, with countries working out trade agreements between each other and exchanging currency or borrowing money.

5. The teacher may place a trade embargo on a country at any given time. The selection of these countries is done at random. Countries experiencing a trade embargo must refrain from trading with other countries until the embargo is lifted.

After the trading:

Students discuss the World Fair and consider the following questions:

What countries did you trade with? Why?

What countries did you not trade with? Why?

What countries were the most difficult to trade with?

What countries were the easiest to trade with?

How did it feel to have lots of money to trade with?

How did it feel to have less money to trade with?

What countries are left in debt? How does it feel?

Which country was prevented from trading at all? How did it feel to be rejected by everyone?

How did it feel to reject this country?

If this is a representation of world trading, what can you say about trade in general?

What can you say about trade between powerful and less powerful countries?

TAKING ACTION: SAMPLE ACTIVITIES

PURPOSE

- to assist students to make links between their understandings and their experience in the real world
- to enable students to make choices and develop the belief that they can be effective participants in society
- to provide further insight into students' understandings for future unit planning

30 Trading day

Set up a trading day or 'swap meet' for students in the school. Encourage students to bring unwanted items that could be traded and exchanged. Involve parents in setting up the day and overseeing the negotiations. Develop a list of regulations governing the transactions. Students could devise formal agreements or contracts to seal the exchange.

31 Thinking about buying

Students reflect on the rules that should govern trade' or exchanges in their personal lives. Ask students to think about what they would take into account in selecting and buying contents for a house. Students put together a shopping list and defend their choices.

Figure 42 *Active participation in the trading process helped consolidate understandings about international exchange*

32 Action plans

Students consider ways in which trade can be used to improve the economies and quality of life for people. They select a country in which people are currently suffering from, for example, food shortage, drought or civil war. They devise an action plan using trade as a mechanism to assist the country.

33 Trade not aid

Students discuss the meaning behind the phrase 'trade, not aid' and devise slogans, posters etc. to communicate their own ideas to others.

34 Putting you in the picture

Using the strategy outlined in chapter 3, students reflect on the implications of their learning about trade on their own lives.

MAPPING UNDERSTANDINGS

Label the countries you know.
Now make a list of products you think are produced in each country.

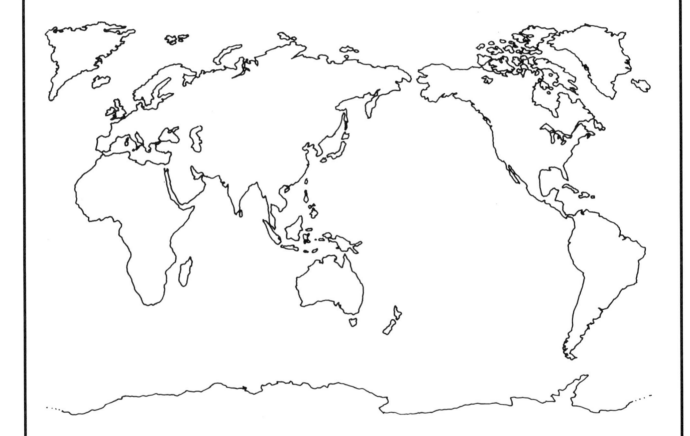

VIETNAM: A CASE STUDY

Vietnam is located in South-East Asia. Much of the country is covered in forest and there is a huge network of rivers which runs throughout the country. Many people live around the Red River in the North and the Mekong Delta in the South. The climate is tropical, with temperatures reaching 38°C in summer and 15°C in the north in winter. The total population of Vietnam in 1993 was 70,400,000.

There has been much conflict in Vietnam during the 20th century. A war between Vietnam and the United States began in 1961 and lasted until 1973. Australia also participated in this war, which cost many lives and left Vietnam in ruin. After the war ended the United States placed a *trade embargo* on Vietnam. This means that it refused to trade with Vietnam. Also, the United States was successful in preventing the World Bank from lending money to Vietnam after the War. This left Vietnam with many debts. This was all changed in 1993 and now Vietnam can borrow money from the World Bank to try to pay off its debts. This money will help the country rebuild its economy and establish trading agreements with many foreign countries.

After the war, Vietnam closed itself off from many foreign countries. Now it has started to open up, and foreign countries are trading with Vietnam and setting up companies in Vietnam. Vietnam exports oil, rice, coffee, tea, textiles, clothing and seafood and in recent years its economy has begun to improve. In 1992 Vietnam achieved a small *trade surplus.* This means that it made a profit from its exports to other countries. Vietnam's major trading partners are Singapore, Japan, Hong Kong, Taiwan, France and the Republic of Korea. Vietnam is also increasing its trade with China.

Vietnam is one of Australia's top twenty-five trading partners. Australia is in the middle range of Vietnam's trading partners. Australia exports telecommunications equipment and metals to Vietnam. In future, it will export aviation equipment, mining equipment, wheat , wool and equipment for agriculture. It will also export equipment to build roads, railways, bridges and so on. Vietnam exports seafood and petroleum to Australia. In the future it is hoped that Vietnam will import services from Australia and students and tourists will come to Australia from Vietnam.

Ref: Dept. of Foreign Affairs and Trade, Australia 1994

INTERNATIONAL TRADE DATA

COUNTRY	TRADING IN THE 1990s	EXPORTS	IMPORTS	MAIN COUNTRIES TRADED WITH
United Kingdom	1992	$US190,052 million manufactured goods, machinery and transportation equipment, fuels and chemicals	$US222,655 million manufactured goods , fuels, food, beverages	European countries, United States of America
The Netherlands	1992	$US139,944 million agricultural products, processed foods, natural gas, metal, textiles and clothing	$US 134,475 million transportation equipment, oil, food products	Germany, Belgium, France, United Kingdom.
Spain	1991	$US59,363 million food, live animals, wood, shoes, machinery, chemicals	$US 93,867 million petroleum, shoes, machinery, chemicals, grain, coffee, iron and steel, cotton	European countries, United States of America, Middle East, Japan, Mexico, United Kingdom, Russian Federation
Russian Federation	1992	$US39,900 million oil and gas, machinery, textiles, chemicals	$US35,000 million textiles, chemicals, machinery	Germany, Italy, United States of America, France, Japan, Netherlands, Finland
Zimbabwe	1990	$US1,726 million tobacco, agricultural products, gold, cotton	$US2,124 million machinery and transportation equipment, chemicals, fuels	Germany, United Kingdom, South Africa, United States of America, Botswana
India	1991	$US17,366 million gems and jewellery, cotton goods, tea	$US20,252 million petroleum, machinery, iron and steel	Russian Federation, United States of America, Japan, Germany, United Kingdom, Belgium, Saudi Arabia

COUNTRY	TRADING IN THE 1990s	EXPORTS	IMPORTS	MAIN COUNTRIES TRADED WITH
China	1992	$US84,635 million textiles, oil	$US80,315 million machinery and transport equipment, iron and steel	Hong Kong, United States of America, Germany, Canada
South Korea	1991	$US71,870,121 million textiles, clothing, shoes, steel, cars, ships	$US81,524,856 million machinery, oil, chemicals, grains	United States of America, Japan, Australia
Australia	1991	$US53,607 million coal, cereals, petroleum, meat, textiles and fibres	$US53,361 million machinery and transport equipment, petroleum products	Japan, United States of America, New Zealand, South Korea, Singapore, Taiwan, Hong Kong, United Kingdom, Germany
United States of America	1992	$US447,829 million machinery and transport equipment, chemicals, food, live animals, beverages	$US548,295 million machinery and transport equipment, paper, textiles, iron and steel	Japan, Canada, West Germany, Taiwan, Mexico United Kingdom South Korea
Brazil	1991	$US31,622 million coffee, iron ore, soya bean, cocoa bean	$US21,010 million mineral and chemical products, oil and appliances	United States of America, The Netherlands, Japan, Germany, Italy, Argentina, Iraq, Saudi Arabia
Saudi Arabia	1990	$US44,417 million petroleum and petroleum products	$US24,069 million manufactured goods, transportation , equipment construction materials	United States of America, Japan, United Kingdom, Germany, Switzerland, Italy

References and further reading

Aguis, R. et al. 1992, *Active Answers: Practical Ideas for Integrating the Curriculum*, Oxford University Press, Melbourne.

Australian Capital Territory Schools Authority (n.d.), *Reading/Writing: Developing Literacy*, Canberra Literacy Program, unit 2, ACT Schools Authority, Canberra.

Babbitt, N. 1975, *Tuck Everlasting*, Farrar Straus Giroux, New York.

Brady, L. 1979, *Feel, Value, Act: Learning About Values*, Theory and Practice, Prentice Hall, Sydney.

Bruner, J. 1960, *The Process of Education*, Harvard University Press, Cambridge.

Bruner, J. 1970, *Man: A Course of Study (MACOS)*, Curriculum Development Associates, Washington DC.

Casteel, J. 1975, *Value Clarification in the Classroom A Primer*, Goodyear Publication, Pacific Palisades Cal.

Christie, F. et al. 1990, *Language: A Resource for Meaning*, Harcourt Brace Jovanovich, Sydney.

Cohen, D. 1987, 'The use of concept maps to represent unique thought processes: towards more meaningful learning', *Journal of Curriculum and Supervision*, vol. 2, no. 3.

Collis, M. & Dalton, J. 1991, *Becoming Responsible Learners: Strategies for Positive Classroom Management*, Eleanor Curtain, Melbourne. (1991, Heinemann, Portsmouth NH.)

Comber, B. 1993, 'Classroom explorations in critical literacy', *Australian Journal of Language and Literacy*, vol. 16, no. 1, pp. 73–83.

Country Economic Brief, Vietnam 1994, Department of Foreign Affairs and Trade, Canberra.

Dalton, J. 1985, *Adventures in Thinking*, Nelson, Melbourne. (1985, Heinemann, Portsmouth NH.)

Dalton, J. & Smith, D 1992, *Extending Children's Special Abilities: Strategies for Primary Classrooms*, Department of School Education, Melbourne.

De Bono, E. 1976, *CoRT Thinking I–IV*, Pergamon Press, London.

De Bono, E. 1985, *Six Thinking Hats*, Penguin, Harmondsworth. (International Centre for Creative Thinking, Larchmont NY.)

Derewianka, B. 1990, *Exploring How Texts Work*, PETA, Sydney.

Dibella, M. & Hamston, J. 1989, *Undercover: Exploring Values Through Children's Literature*, Collins Dove, Melbourne.

Donaldson, M. 1978, *Children's Minds*, Fontana, London.

Dubosarsky, U. 1993, *The Last Week in December*, Penguin, Melbourne.

Dufty, H. & Dufty, D. 1990, *Literacy for Life: Integrating Learning in the Classroom*, School and Community, Dellasta, Melbourne.

Ferret, M. 1990, *Learning to Discover*, Martin Education, Sydney.

Goodman, K., Goodman, Y. & Hood, W. (eds) 1989, *The Whole Language Evaluation Book*, Heinemann, Portsmouth NJ.

Freire, P. & Macedo, D. 1987, *Literacy: Reading the Word and the World*, Bergin & Garvey, South Hadley Mass.

Giroux, H. 1987, 'Critical literacy and student experience: Donald A Graves' approach to literacy', *Language Arts*, vol. 64, no. 2, pp. 175–81.

Giroux, H. 1988, *Teachers as Intellectuals: Towards a Critical Pedagogy of Learning*, Bergin & Garvey, Granby Mass.

Greig, S. et al. 1987, *Earth Rights: Education as if the Planet Really Mattered*, Kogan Page, London.

Hamston, J. 1994, *To Market, To Market: Local and International Markets*, Macmillan, Melbourne.

Hamston, J. Pigdon, K. & Woolley, M. 1995, *To Market*, Curriculum Corporation, Melbourne,

Hancock, J. & Leaver, C. 1994, *Major Teaching Strategies for English*, ARA, Melbourne.

Hill, S. & Hill, T. 1990, *The Collaborative Classroom*, Eleanor Curtain, Melbourne.

Hornsby, D., Parry, J. & Sukarna, D. 1992, *Teach On: Teaching Strategies for Reading and Writing Workshops*, Phoenix Education, Melbourne.

'Korea: land of morning calm' 1988, *Asia Teacher Bulletin* (special edn), vol. 16, no. 1.

Kress, G. & Knapp, P. 1992, 'Genre in a social theory of language', *English in Education*, vol. 26, no. 2, pp. 4–15.

Luke, A. 1991, 'Literacies as social practices', *English Education*, October, pp. 131–47.

Mathews, B. & Cleary, P. 1993, *The Integrated Curriculum In Use*, Ashton Scholastic, Sydney.

Ministry of Education 1985, *Destination Decisions: Decision Making for School Communities*, Ministry of Education, Melbourne.

Murdoch, K. 1992, *Integrating Naturally*, Dellasta, Melbourne.

Murdoch, K. 1993, *Springboards: Ideas for Environmental Education*, Nelson, Melbourne. (1993, Heinemann, Portsmouth NH.)

Murdoch, K 1996, *Voyages Across the Curriculum*, Nelson, Melbourne.

Patterson, R. 1991, 'Teaching how to read the world and change it: critical pedagogy in the intermediate grades', in *Literacy as Praxis: Culture, Language and Pedagogy*, ed. C. Walsh, Ablex, Norwood, NJ.

Pigdon, K. & Woolley, M. (eds) 1992, *The Big Picture: Integrating Children's Learning*, Eleanor Curtain, Melbourne. (1992, Heinemann, Portsmouth NH.)

Pike, G. & Selby, D. 1988, *Global Teacher, Global Learner*, Hodder & Stoughton, London. (1988, Lubrecht & Cramer, Forestburgh NY.)

Richard, N. 1979, *Springboards: Ideas for Social Studies*, Nelson, Melbourne.

Rodda, E. 1990, *Finders Keepers*, Omnibus, Norwood SA. (1990, Harcourt Brace, New York.)

Roddick, A. 1992, *Body and Soul*, Vermillion, London.

Singh, R. 1991, *Values Education for the Twenty-First Century: Asia-Pacific Perspectives*, UNESCO, New York.

Snowball, D. & Hammond, A. 1991, *Integrating Learning: Planned Integrated Units*, Bookshelf Publishing Australia, Gosford, NSW.

Stauffer, R. 1970, *The Language Experience Approach to the Teaching of Reading*, Harper & Row, New York.

Stewart-Dore, N. & Morris, B. 1984, *Learning to Learn from Text: Effective Reading in the Content Areas*, Addison-Wesley, Sydney.

Viviani, N. 1991, 'Asian studies for Australian schools the critical questions: why, what, how?' ETHOS: Journal of the Social Studies Teacher, annual, pp. 7–11.

Wilson, J. & Wing Jan, L. 1993, *Thinking for Themselves*, Eleanor Curtain, Melbourne. (1993, Heinemann, Portsmouth NH.)

Wilson, L. et al. 1991, *An Integrated Curriculum Approach to Learning*, Nelson, Melbourne.

Wing Jan, L, 1991, *Write Ways*, Oxford University Press, Melbourne.

More Books from Heinemann

The Big Picture
Integrating Students' Learning
Edited by Marilyn Woolley and Keith Pigdon

The Big Picture addresses the key issues which are central to the idea of the integrated curriculum and translates them into practical classroom advice.
   Contents: Context and framework: the ideas which drive teachers' curriculum planning; a planning model: bringing the components together in an organised yet flexible structure; the model in practice: activities and strategies; language and the integrated curriculum: integrated learning and specific curriculum practice; assessment and evaluation: for the learner, the teacher and the community; whole school change: it starts in your classroom.
   ISBN 0 435 08792 4   illustrated 128 pp

Thinking for Themselves
Developing Strategies for Reflective Learning
Jeni Wilson and Lesley Wing Jan

By encouraging children to think about their learning and to become aware of and control their thinking processes, teachers can help them become active, responsible learners who can make their own decisions, choose appropriate strategies, assess their own work and set their own goals.
   Contents: getting started; developing the appropriate learning environment; program planning; negotiating with students; questioning and self-assessment techniques.
   ISBN 0 435 08805 X   illustrated 156 pp

Responsive Evaluation
Making Valid Judgments about Student Literacy
Edited by Brian Cambourne and Jan Turbill

Changes in teaching practice caused by new understandings of how children learn have made many traditional methods of evaluation obsolete. Demands to demonstrate accountability put pressure on teachers to devise new methods of assessment which demonstrate accountability and are appropriate to current teaching methods.
   Responsive Evaluation presents approaches which lead to optimum learning, reflect holistic thinking, enrich classroom teaching and are seen to be rigorous, scientific and valid.
   Jan Turbill and Brian Cambourne have worked with teachers, principals, academics, parents and students to establish assessment procedures. All have contributed to *Responsive Evaluation* and report on how they put the theory into practice.
ISBN 0 435 08829 7   illustrated 176 pp

ISBN   0 435 08820 3   illustrated   96 pp

For information on these and other titles contact
Heinemann
361 Hanover Street, Portsmouth, NH 03801-3912
Tel 603- 431 7894   Fax 603- 431 7840